#ShareMondays 2019

The third annual photobook of winning images from the weekly twitter competition which is run uniquely by the online photography community. With no marketing strategies or agendas this competition throws up a wonderful diverse collection of work from extremely talented photographers.

www.sharemondays.co.uk

Foreward by Mark Littlejohn
@mark_lj

I've always felt that there are huge swathes of incredibly talented photographers out there that never get any sort of recognition of any kind. None. I see various photographers receiving national and international acclaim and I often think that the only difference between them and countless others is opportunity. Is it that they have a better business head or separate funds to allow them to travel to Hokkaido or Huangshan or wherever and spend several months with nothing else to do than take photographs. The vast majority of photographers would just love the time, never mind the opportunity to go to far-flung exotic shores. The advent of social media has helped bring more wonderfully talented people to the attention of a wider audience. The likes of instagram, twitter and Facebook have in the region of 4 billion users alone (although I'm assuming there will be one or two doublers) in there. But even then there are so many unique and individual photographers out there with just a handful of followers. How do you get noticed? Do you want to get noticed? I've always been happiest just doing my own thing and probably my most used phrase is "I couldn't give a bugger". And that's true to a certain extent. You have to follow your heart. You have to take your own photos not someone else's. You only need to please one person. But it's nice to be loved. It's nice to see your art being appreciated by others, even if you are a grumpy bugger who says they don't care. If you are proud of an image it's a good feeling to see it get the plaudits it deserves. And that's why I think that ShareMondays is a wonderful initiative. It's almost "by the people for the people". It helps to get your images to a wider audience. There is a simple hash tag to check each week and see what everyone has been up to. Who is new, who has changed direction, who has knocked one out the park. Again. I think the approach where each winner judges the following weeks competition is inspired. It allows for a more eclectic selection assortment of images. And because its chosen by the people who take part you know that it's not being run with any agenda other than the love of a shared passion. I've loved looking through the winning entries. There are so many favourites. It really is a lovely book, full of individuality. Everyone who has had a part in it should feel rightly proud. Seeing your work in print, either hung on your wall or in a beautiful book, is just the most satisfying feeling.

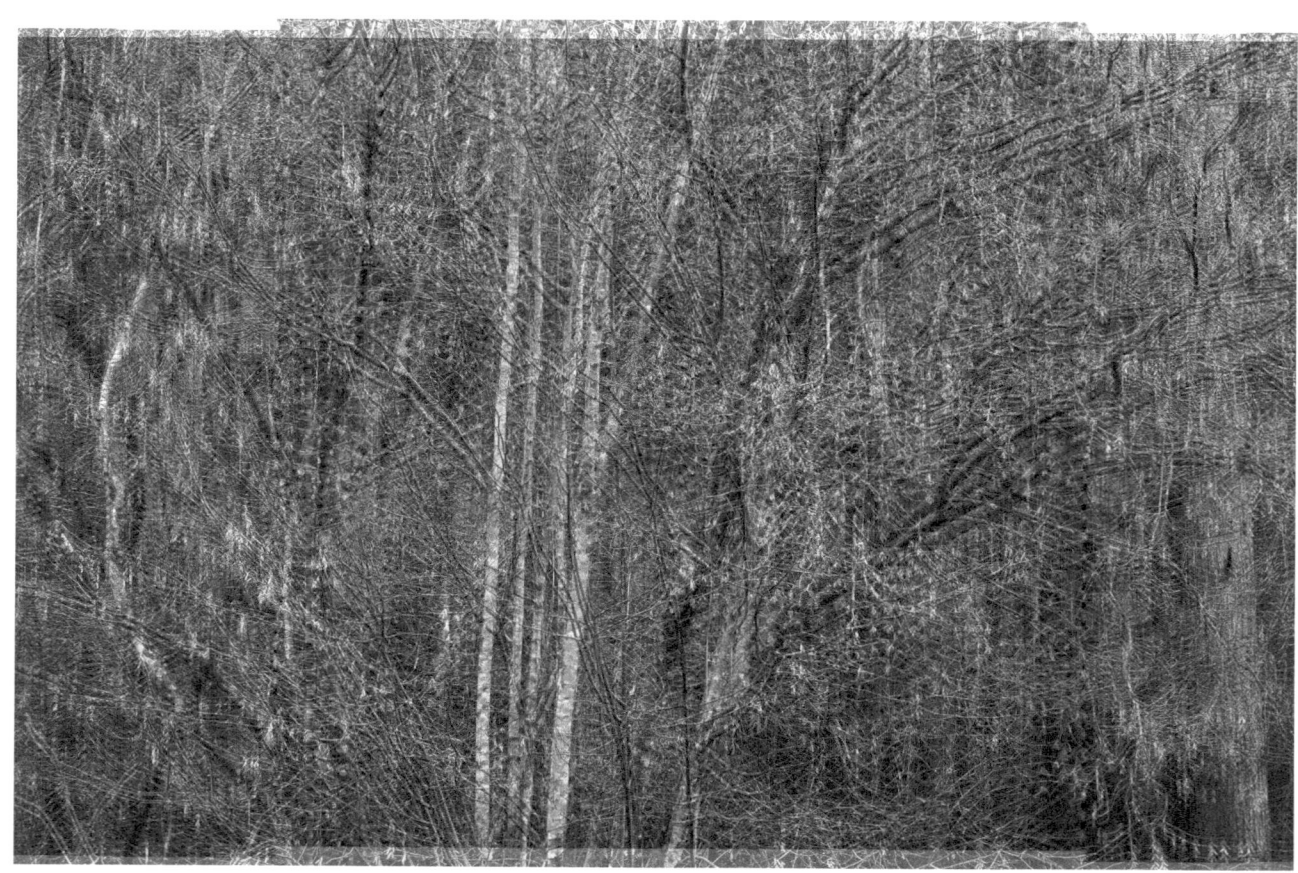

Chaos & Order by Claire Ashmore

An image taken in the Forest of Dean, with the chaos of the emerging branches and catkins softening the order from the trunks in the heart of the image.

Fuji XT1 XC50-230@50mm f5.0 and 1/30sec ISO 200

Judged by Steve Palmer

Week 1

Lakeside Reeds by Darren Rose

An early morning at the local lake, just before the sun came up. Everything was calm and still, and it was a lovely way to start the day.

Leica M10, Leica Summicron 90mm f/2 @ f/8, 1/25s and ISO100. Tripod

Judged by Claire Ashmore

Week 2

The Pied Pier by Will Mallett

After a long (and cold) walk on the Gog Magog Hills just outside of Cambridge, the children had had enough and wanted to go home. That was until they saw someone practising bubbles on the hill. A sudden burst of energy and they were off. My daughter can be seen running to the left of the image. Image taken on an Canonet Q17 Giii using Ilford PanF+ pushed one stop. Settings long forgotten.

Judged by Darren Rose

Week 3

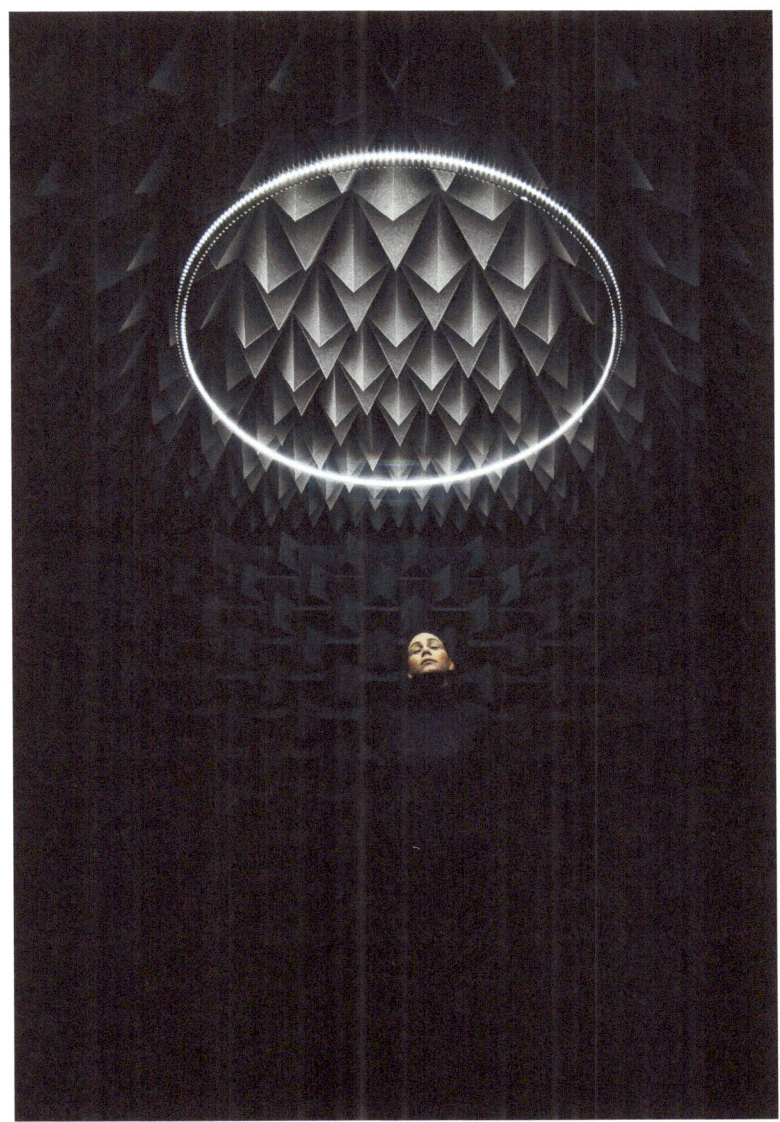

Chamber by James Benwell

Taken inside Haroon Mirza's "The National Apavillion of Then And Now" - an anechoic chamber which reflects neither light nor sound, its circle of light grows in brightness along with an ever-increasing sonic buzz, before suddenly plunging the space back into darkness and silence.
Nikon D750 Tokina 16-28mm f2.8 @ f2.8 1/60s ISO 1600
Judged by Will Mallett
Week 4

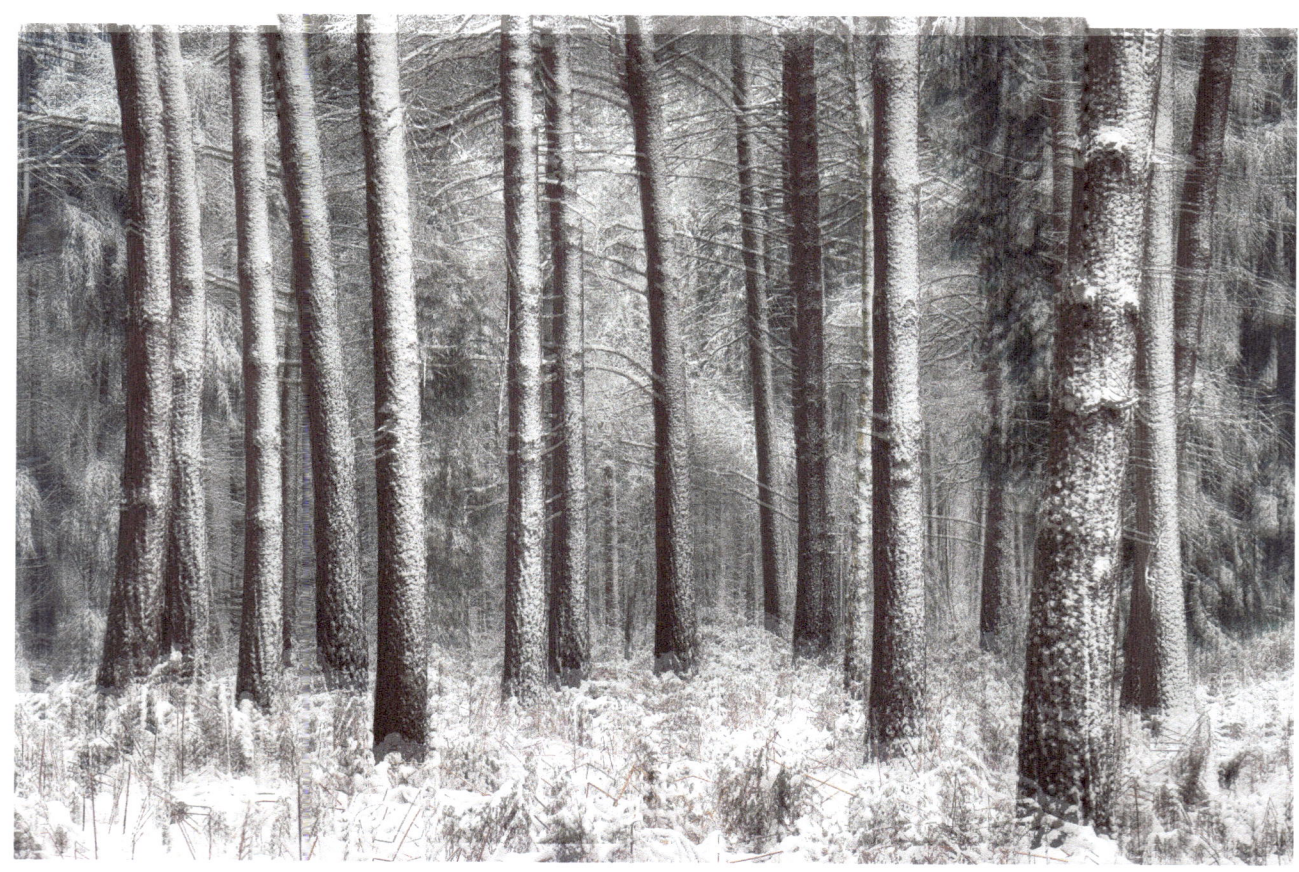

The Gathering by Amar Sood

It had been a meagre winter with not much in the way of snow, frost, mist or light. So when I saw a modest overnight snowfall in the forecast, I became unduly excited and packed my bag for an early morning start. I decided to head to a dense woodland which I knew would look uniform in snow for as long as possible before it melted. After getting my eye in, I stumbled across this group of trees. A wall of uniformity broken up and saved from a chaotic environment of the woodland.

Sony A7rII, Sony FE 70-200mm f/4 @ 200mm and f/8 /ISO 100, 1/4s and ISO 100. Handheld

Judged by James Benwell

Week 5

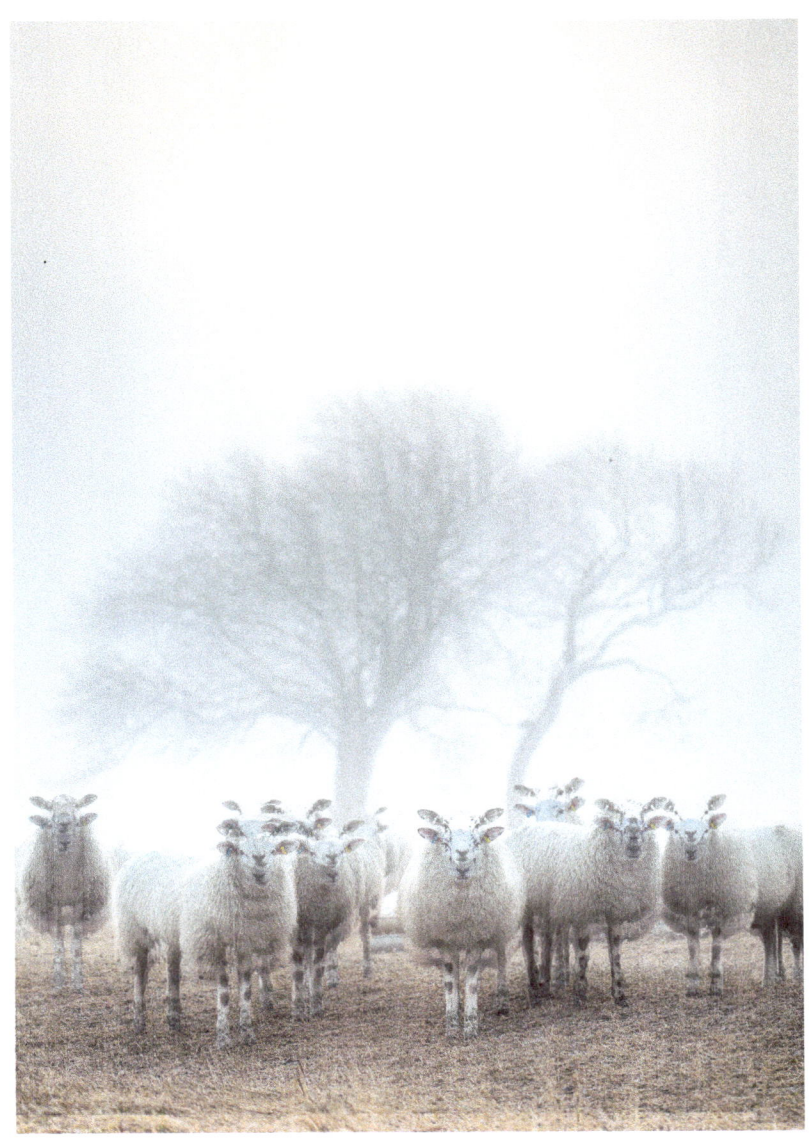

Sheep in the mist by Anita Nicholson
From a quick dash to a field near home before work one morning.
Canon 5DMKIII, Canon 100mm field f/2.8, 1/800s at ISO 100, handheld, no filters.
Judged by Anir Sood
Week 6

Untitled by Daniel Sands

This walkway across the river Stour near my home in Wimborne has always caught my attention - it seems so juxtaposed in it's surroundings and always felt a bit alien to me. I'd been wanting to shoot it for some time, but wanted the right conditions to help portray that alien feeling. In Feb I woke to a very foggy morning and knew the time was right - all I had to do was wait for the right figure to walk into the scene. I've intentionally choose a shot where it's not immediately obvious if the figure is heading toward the camera or away from it, because I want this image to depict a scene of somebody coming out of the unknown, and also somebody walking straight into it (as we all do each day!).

Judged by Anita Nicholson

Week 7

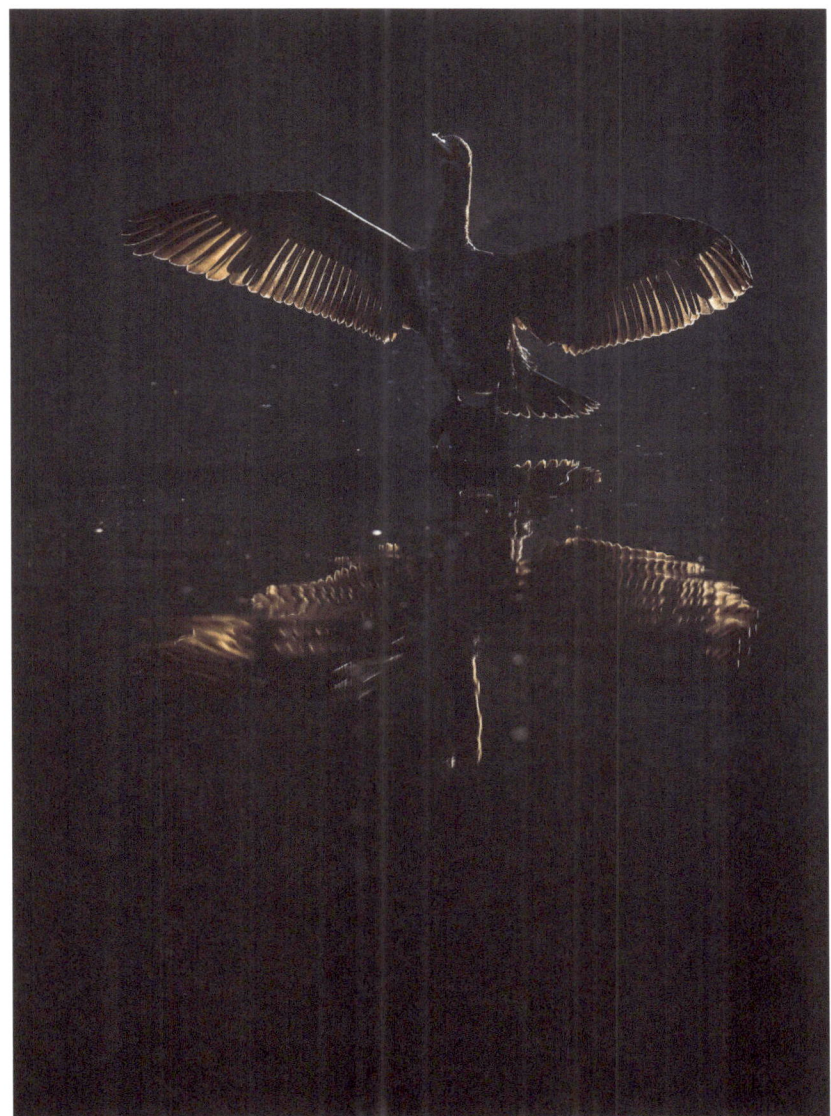

Mirrored Cormorant by Matthew Cattell

I spent the winter of 2018/19 photographing cormorants at a local pool as part of an ongoing 'urban wildlife' project. Being less than 5 minutes from my house I was able to get to know the location and its inhabitants in order to make the most of best light as well as interesting weather conditions.
Nikon D500, Nikon 500mm f4 @ f5.6, 1/800s and ISO 200. Tripod
Judged by Daniel Sands
Week 8

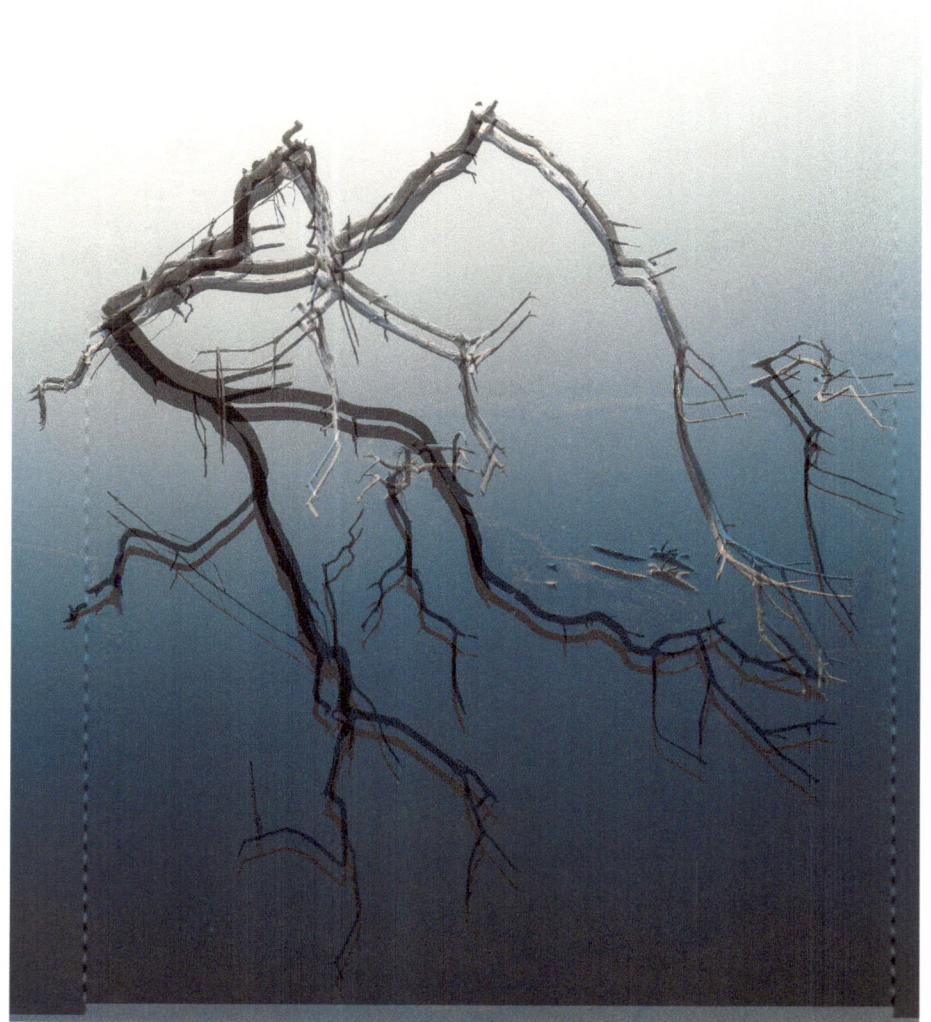

The Rising by Dylan Nardini
A still calm evening at Lunan Bay
Nikon D850, Nikon 24mm VR f/1.4, 1/60th sec, f8 ISO 64
Judged by Matthew Cattell
Week 9

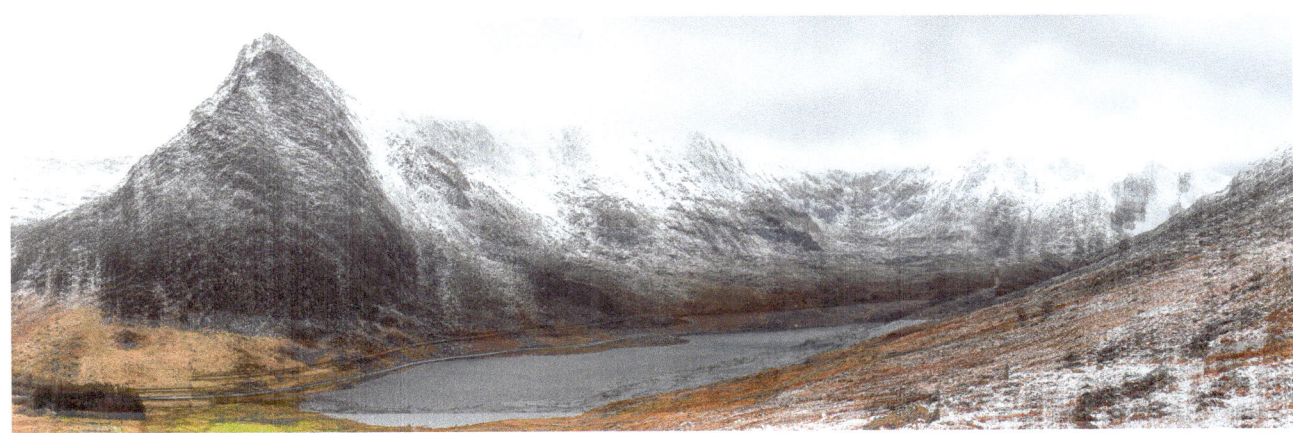

The Glyderau by Amar Sood

This was my first visit to Snowdonia and it's fair to say the weather had not been kind. On the first day the rain was as heavy as I'd ever seen. The second day brought winds which literally knocked me off my feet. The overnight forecast for the third day of the trip was rapidly falling temperatures with heavy overnight rainfall and snow at higher altitudes. I had arranged to meet fellow photographer Ollie Popock with the plan of heading up alongside Llyn Idwal to photograph the Glyderau panorama in full. We knew we wouldn't be on the ground for long so we quickly made our way up to our chosen vantage point. Rather than photograph it alongside Llyn Idwal, I decided to go wide and capture the majesty of the Glyderau with their fresh dusting of snow.

Sony A7rII, Nikon 24-70mm f/2.8 G AF-S @ 48mm f/11 1/60 sec ISO 250. Handheld 8 image vertical panorama

Judged by Dylan Nardini

Week 10

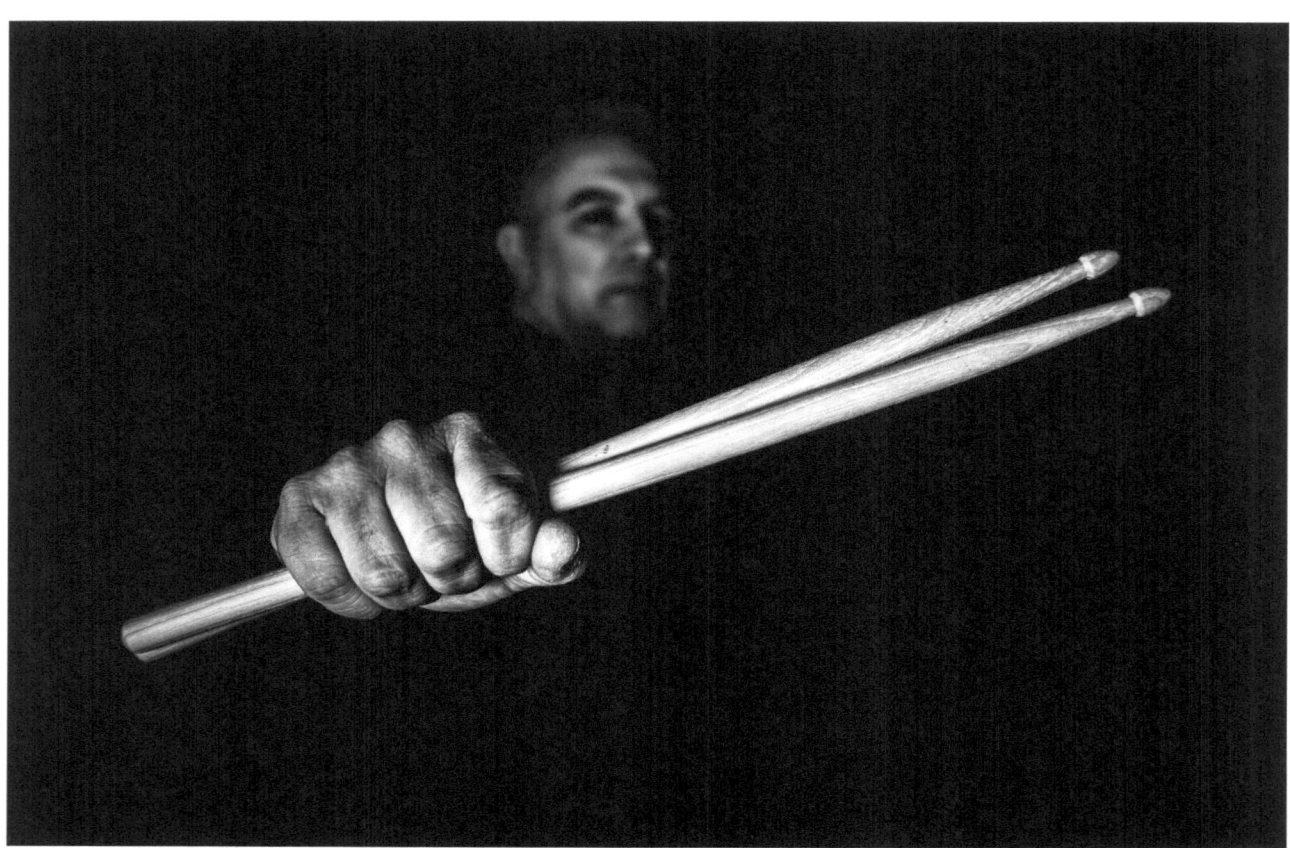

Stick With It by Sarah Longes

From a great photoshoot with drummer Andy Gray. For me, portraiture needs to tell a story. Sometimes a minimalist, subtle image can carry that story in a far more powerful way than a traditional portrait. Andy's drumsticks are an extension of himself, in much the same way as my camera is now, or my brush was when I was painting. When you stick with the thing you love, not just what you do, but who you are, the means by which you choose to express yourself aren't just tools any more. The connection becomes organic. I am my art, Andy is his music!

Fujifilm XT2 with Fujinon 18mm at 18mm, 27mm equivalent, 1/500 f2 ISO 500

Judged by Amar Sood

Week 11

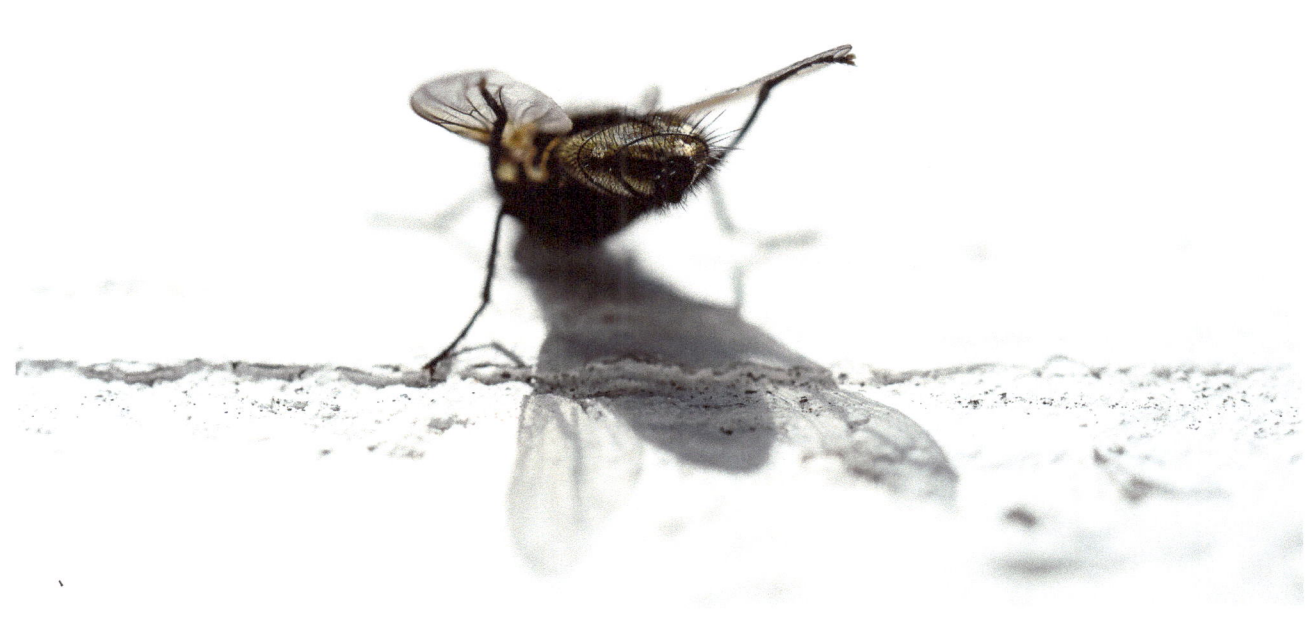

Super Fly by Will Mallett

I was going for the eyes but tried to make the best of it when the little bugger turned around and wiggled its behind at me. I really liked the hairy posterior & unusual pose.
Olympus OMD-em10 mk ii 60mm macro at 3.5 320iso.
Judged by Sarah Longes
Week 12

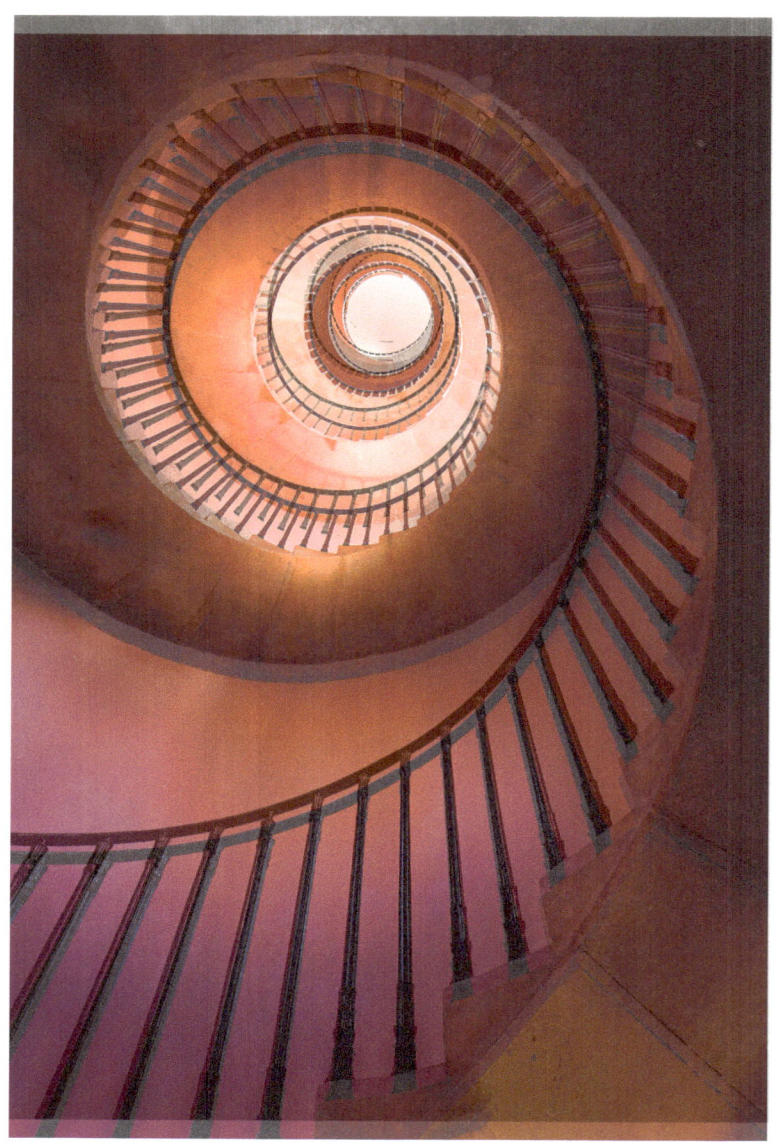

Beckford Tower, Bath by Stu Meech
Nikon D750, Nikon 16-35 f/4 @ f/11, 0.5s and ISO100. Camera propped up by wallet and trigged via phone app.
Judged by Will Mallett
Week 13

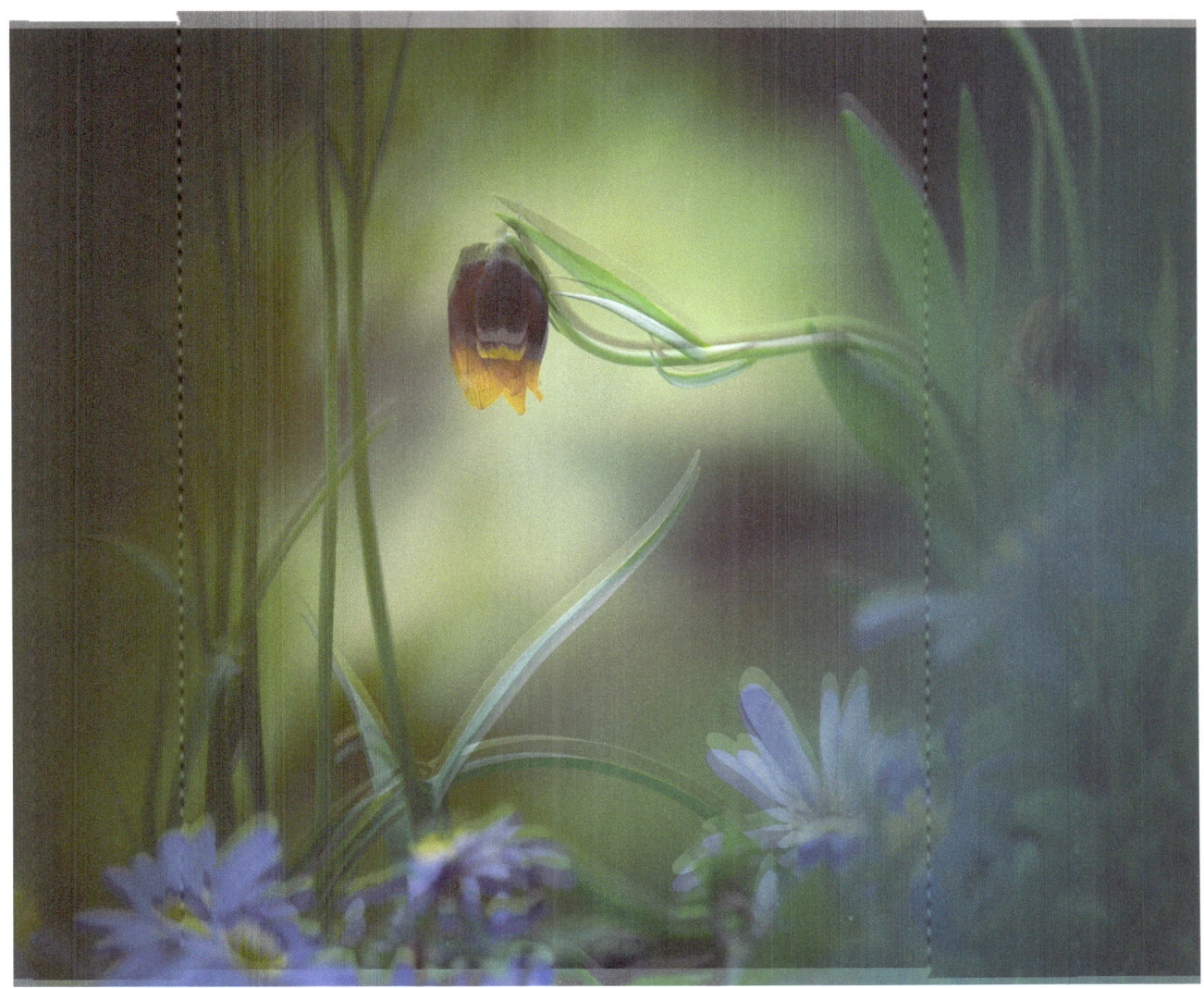

Fritillaria Michailovski by Glenys Garnett
Fuji XT2 Fuji 100-400 f4.5 f5.6 @ 1/250 - ISO 200 Handheld
Judged by Sue Meech
Week 14

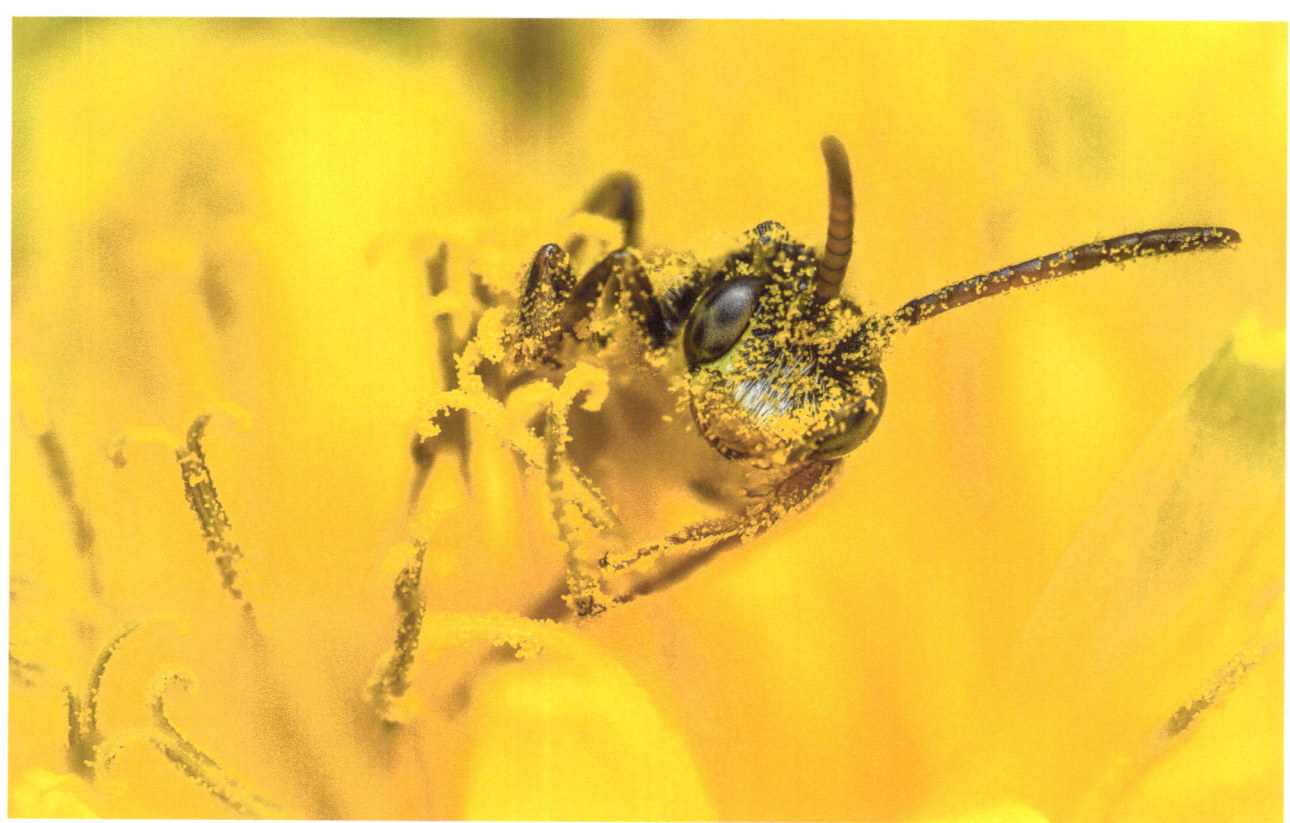

Little Nomad by Phil Savoie

On a crisp April morning along the River Wye a tiny bee harvests Dandelion pollen. At 4.5mm the Little Nomad Bee (Nomada flavoguttata) is one of the smallest of the 270+ UK bee species. Nikon D850 Laowa 25mm Macro 2.5x @ 5.6 80 ISO 1/2500 diffused Nikon SB500 flash 8 shot stack

Judged by Glenys Garnett

Week 15

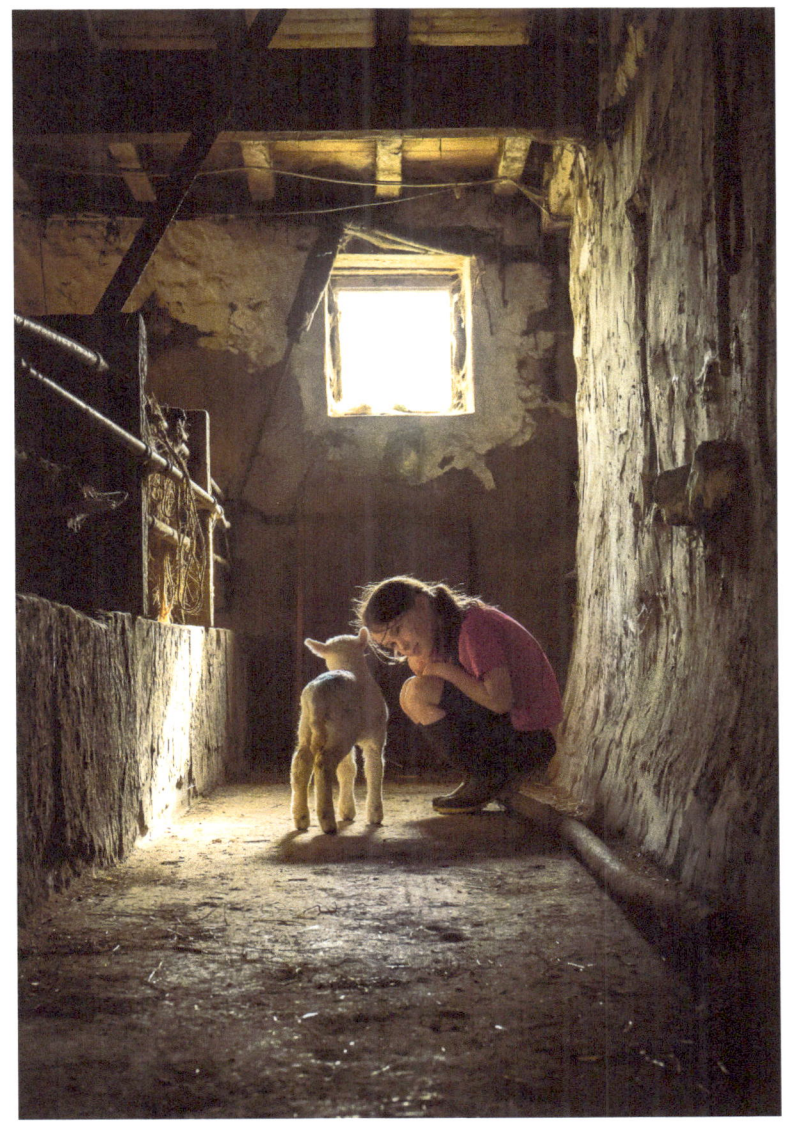

Florence and her Lamb by Amy Bateman

Judged by Phil Savoie
Week 16

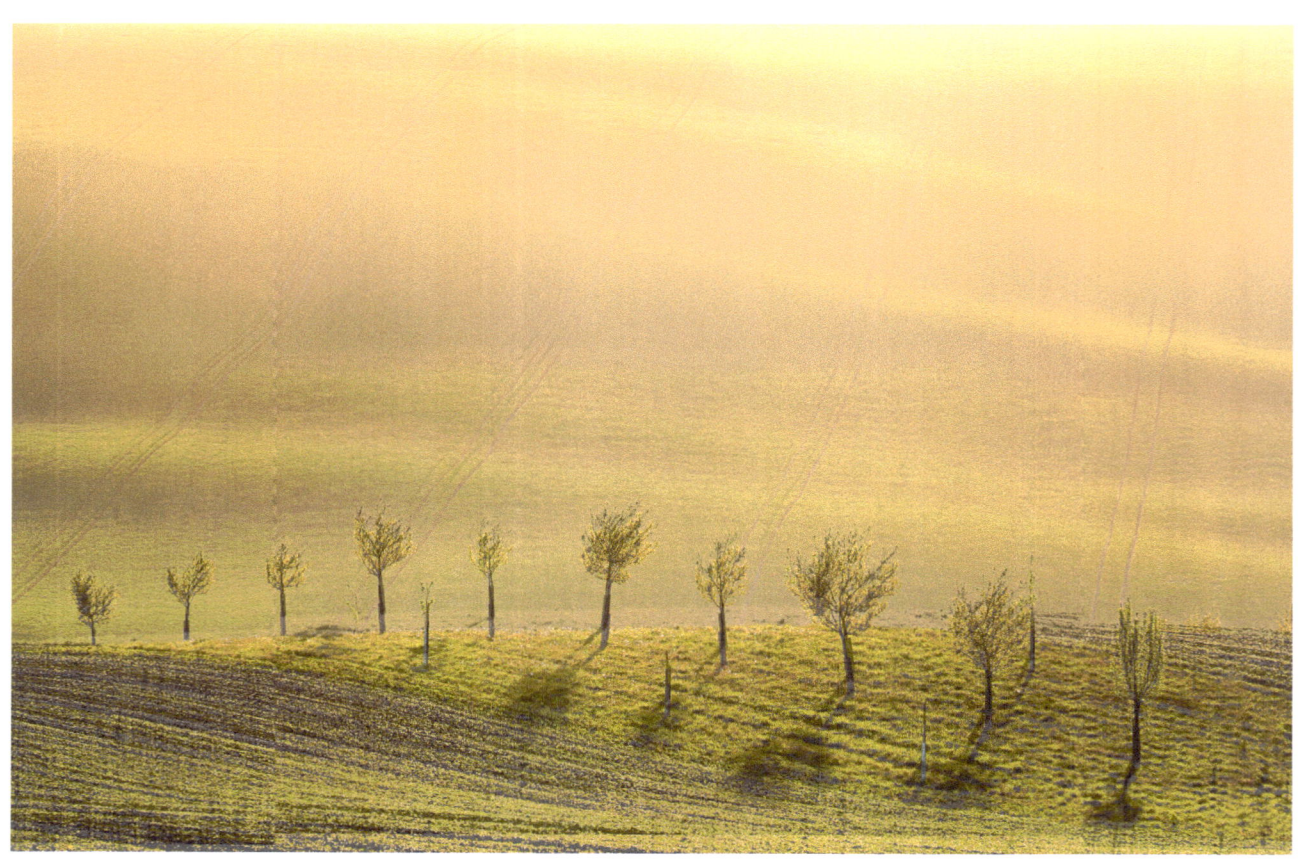

The Wall of Light by Andrew Robertson

Description: Picking out shapes with a long lens as the early morning light hits the rolling hills of South Moravia.
Canon EOS 5D Mark IV, Canon EF100-400mm f/4.5-5.6L IS II USM @263mm f/16 1/10th second ISO 100
Judged by Andy Bateman
Week 17

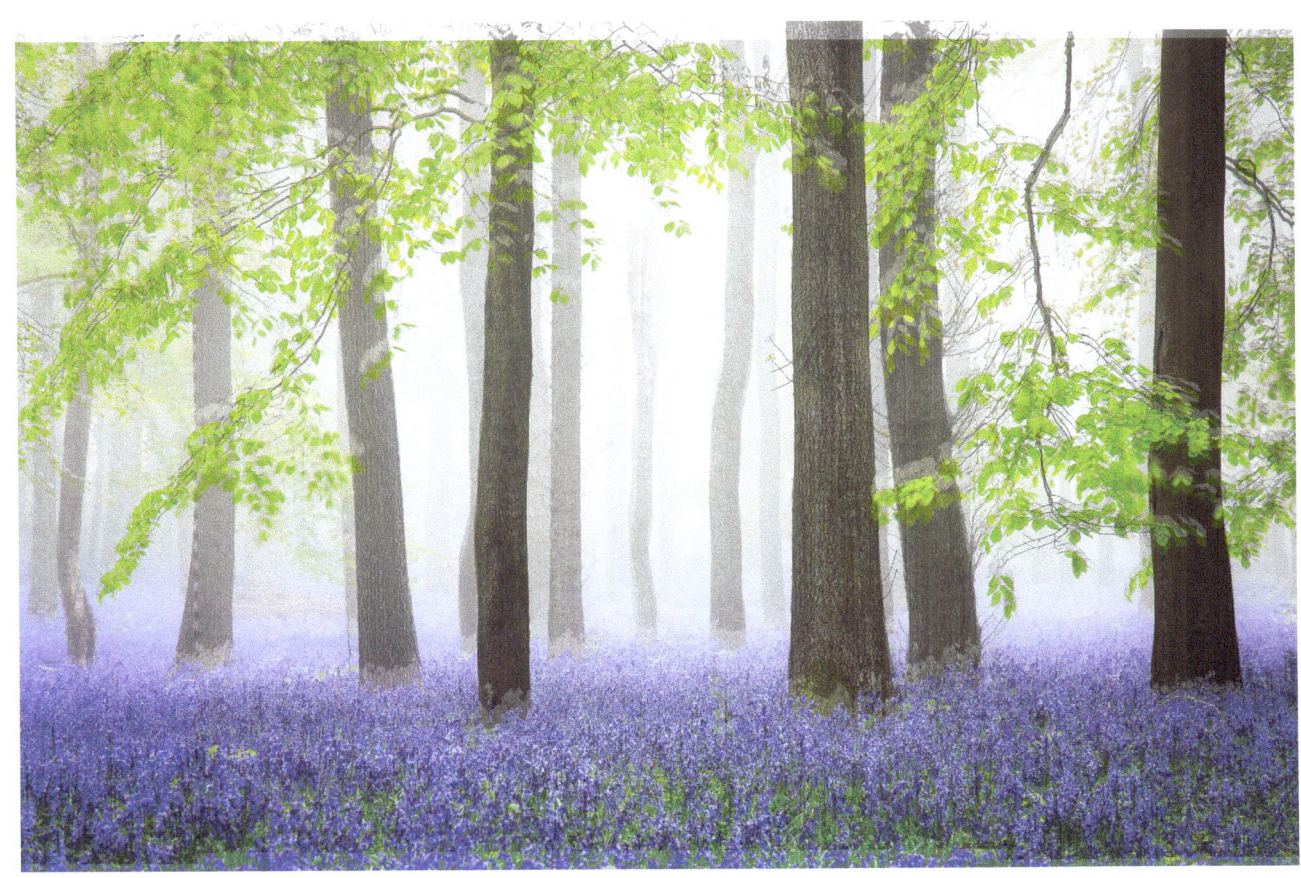

Bluebells by Mandy Davies
Judged by Andrew Robertson
Week 18

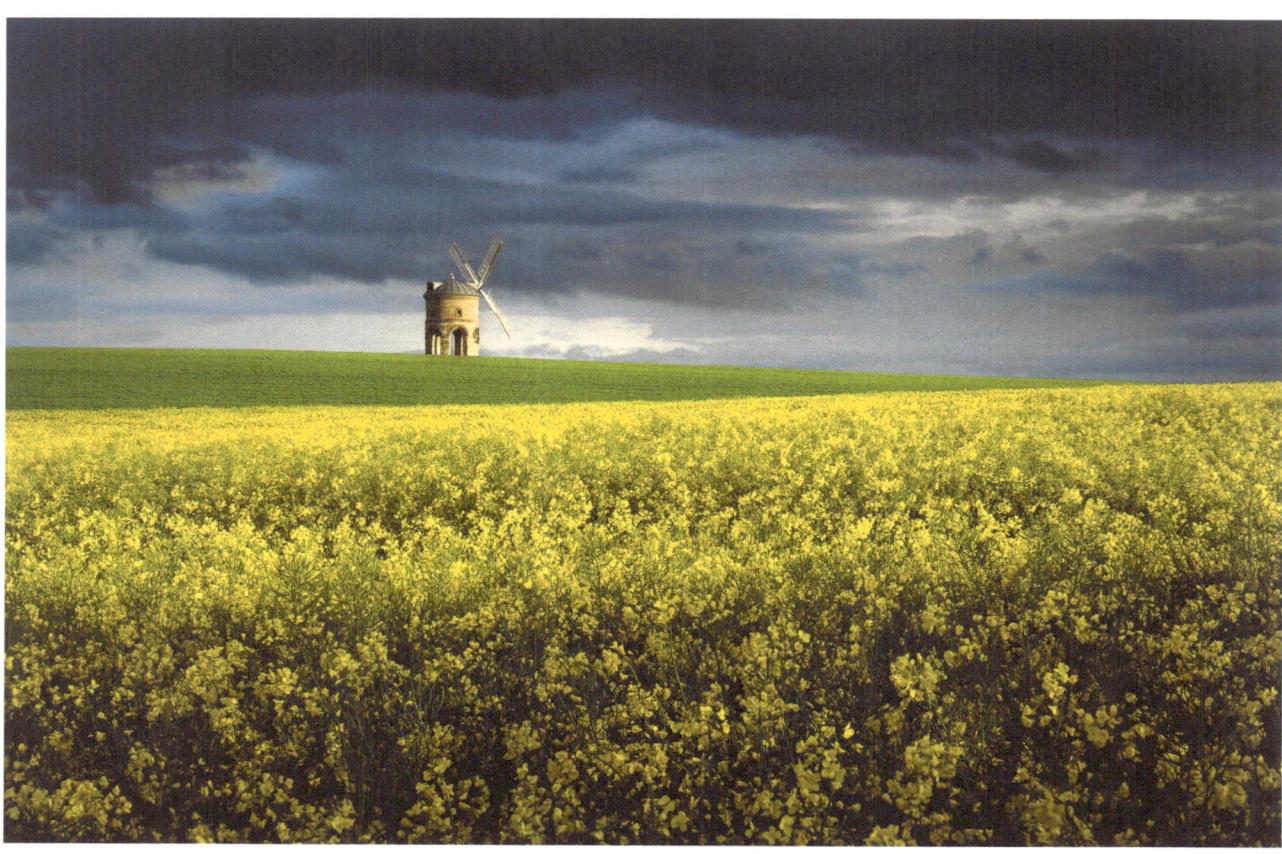

Chesterton Windmill at Spring by Stu Meech
Warwickshire.
Nikon D750, Nikon 24-120mm f/4 @ f/16, 1/30th and ISO400. Tripod & LEEfilters 0.6nd Hard Grad and Landscape Polariser.
Judged by Mandy Davies
Week 19

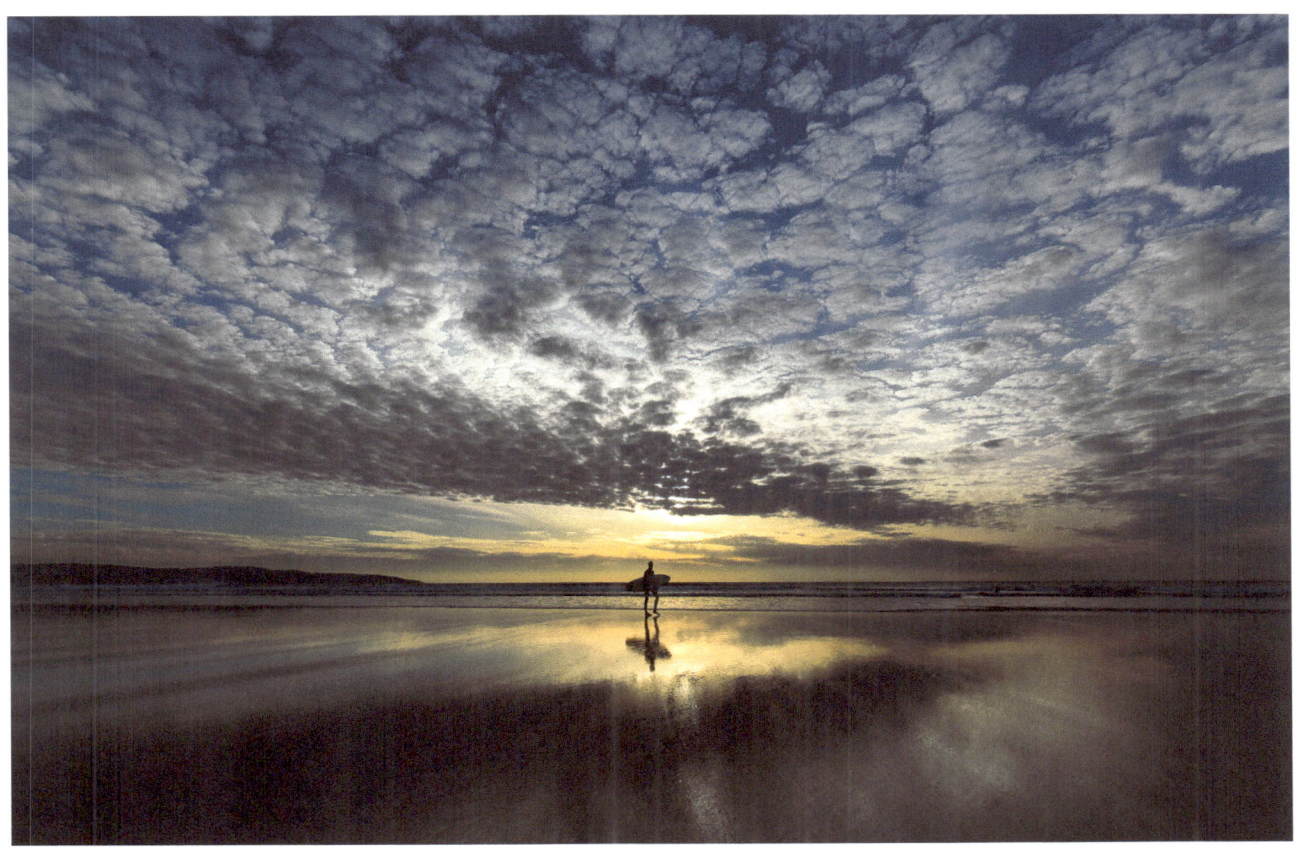

SHANGRI-LA by Ian Lewis

A wonderful evening on Gwithian beach in Cornwall for a camera club field trip. As this surfer left the sea the elements lined up for this shot.
Canon 5D MKIII, Tamron 15-30mm f2.8 @ f16, 1/200s and ISO 100. Tripod and bracketed shot.
Judged by Stu Meech
Week 20

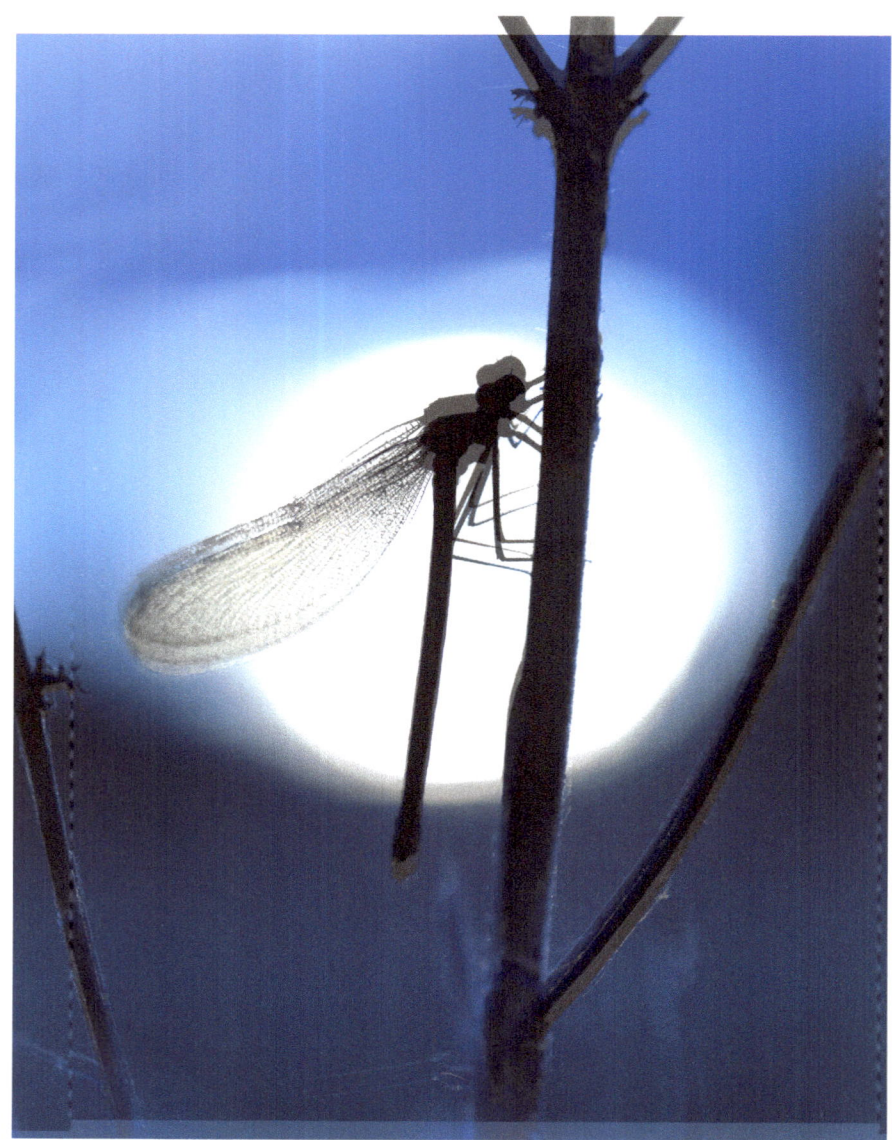

The Roost by Jay Birmingham

A banded demoiselle taken at sunrise. I took the shot at f/2.8 to isolate the subject and to enable the light from the rising sun to form a halo circle behind the silhouetted damselfly.

Canon 6D Mark ii with 100mm lens, 1/4000 sec, f/2.8 at ISO 1000, on tripod

Judged by Ian DeWolf

Week 21

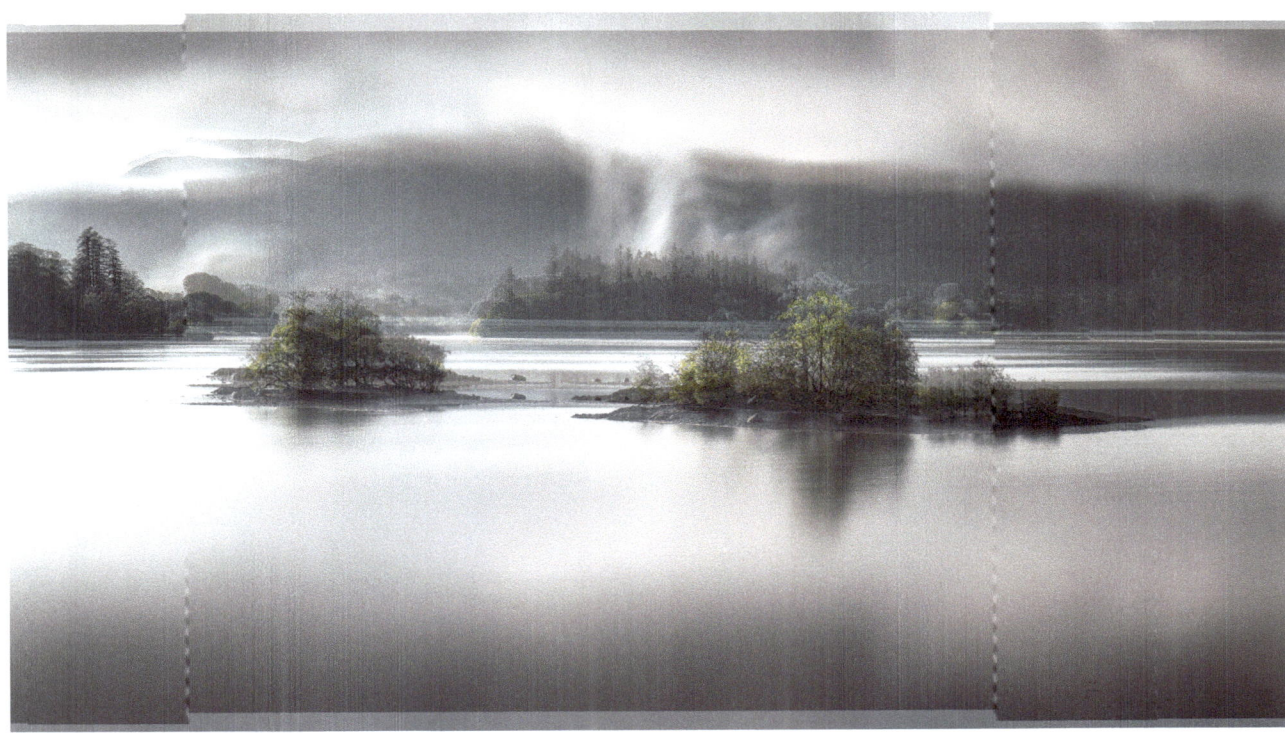

Plume by Pete Wilkinson

The image was captured at sunrise from the balcony of a boathouse in Portinscale, Cumbria. It's a long exposure looking out across Derwent Water, over the Lingholm Islands towards Lord's Island and the Great Wood on the eastern shore. Sony A7RII, Sony FE 24-70mm f4 @ 38mm, 30 seconds, ISO 100. Benro tripod & Lee 10 Stop filter

Judged by Jev Birmingham

Week 22

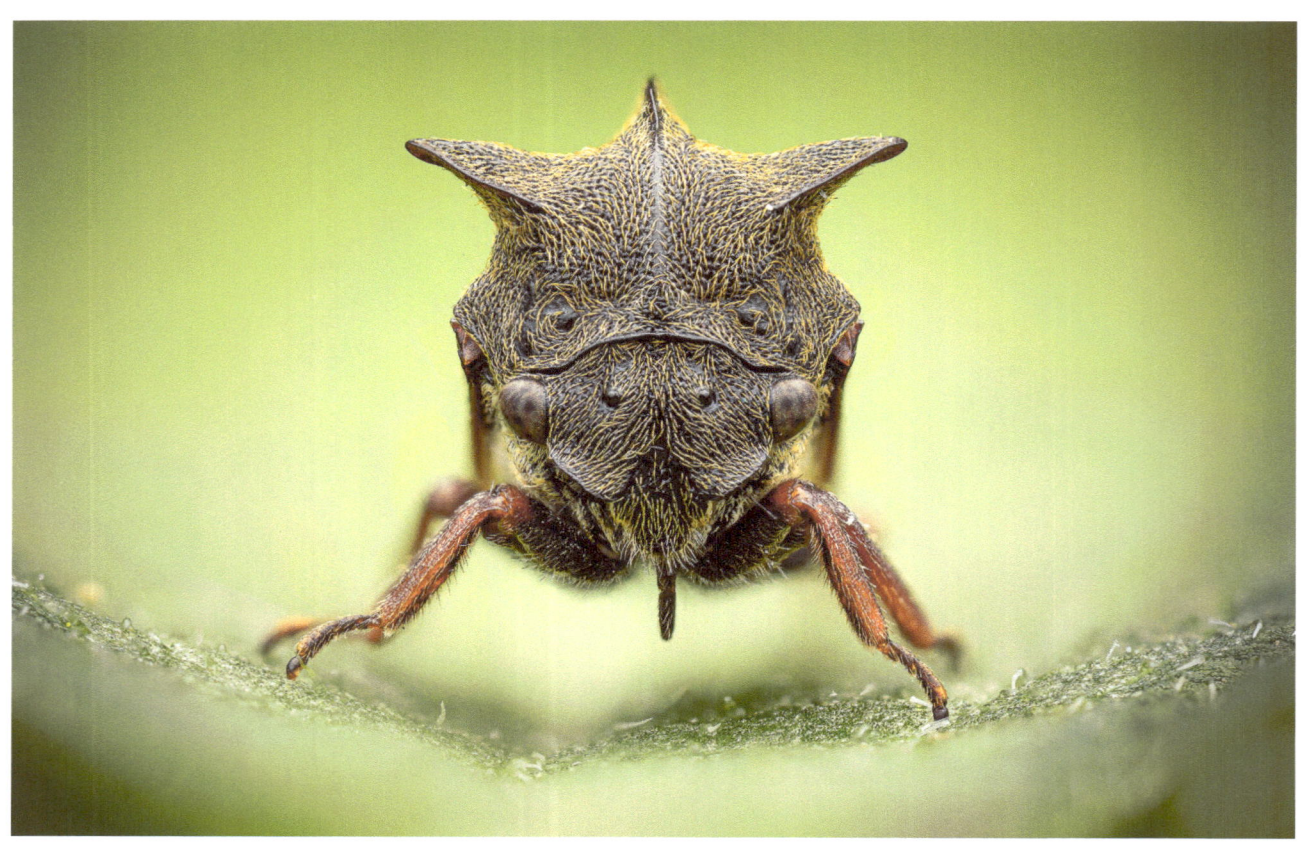

Tree Hopper by Keith Truman
Multi image stack taken with the following Camera / settings
Canon 5D IV Mpe-65mm, Single 580EX II flash with DIY diffuser, Berlebach mini tripod, Newport linear stage ISO200 f5.6 1/125sec
Judged by Pete Wilkinson
Week 23

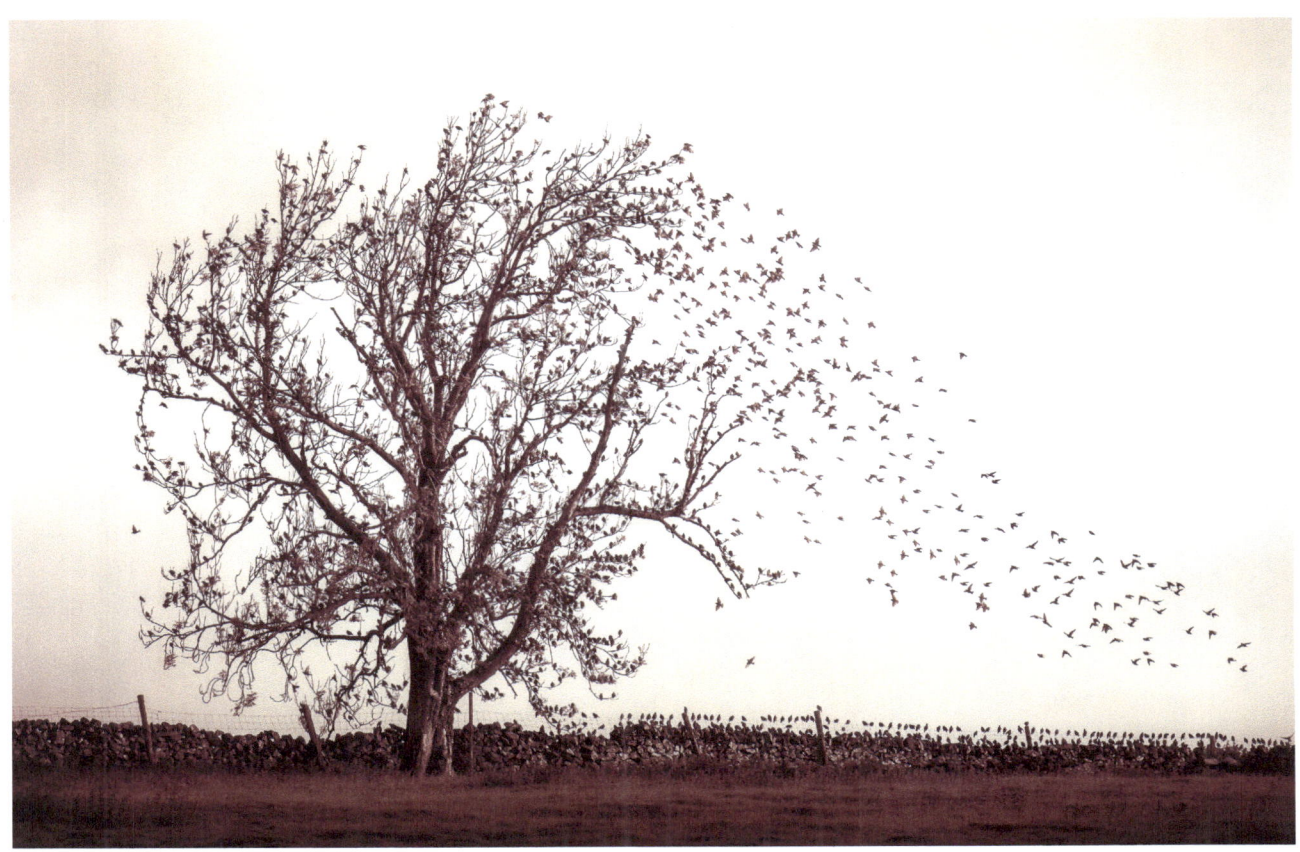

Starlings and the Ash by Paul Howell

Early on a summer's morning the starlings began to stir. I followed them as they moved languidly across Craven Moor. Gathering on a lone, weathered ash they fleetingly appear like falling leaves in an autumn breeze. Fujifilm X-T2, Fujifilm XF55-200mm F3.5-4.8 @ f/7.1, 1/950s, ISO 500, Handheld

Judged by Keith Trueman

Week 24

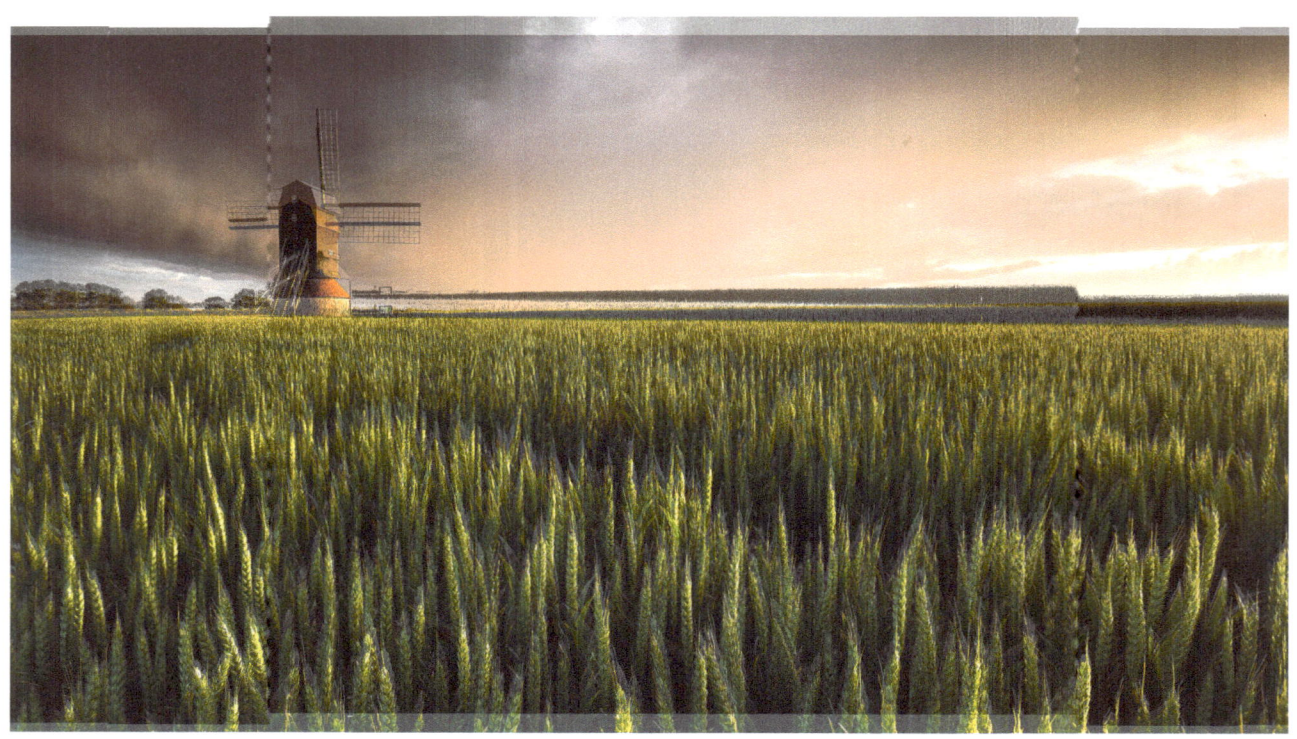

Stevington Windmill by Amar Sood

It was a tempestuous summer evening. The forecast wasn't great, but I had a feeling there would be a break in the cloud around sunset. It was a good opportunity to visit Stevington Windmill, a location which I'd been meaning to get to for some time. Needless to say, I thought I could get there quicker than I did. There was a double rainbow to the north east point I made it, the light was fading fast. There was a break in the cloud and the scene was bathed in golden light. The conditions turned out to be much better than I could have imagined.

Nikon Z7, Nikon Z 24-70mm f/4 S @ 24mm, 1/6 s, f/11, ISO 64. Tripod, Polariser and 3 Stop Soft Grad.

Judged by Paul Howell

Week 25

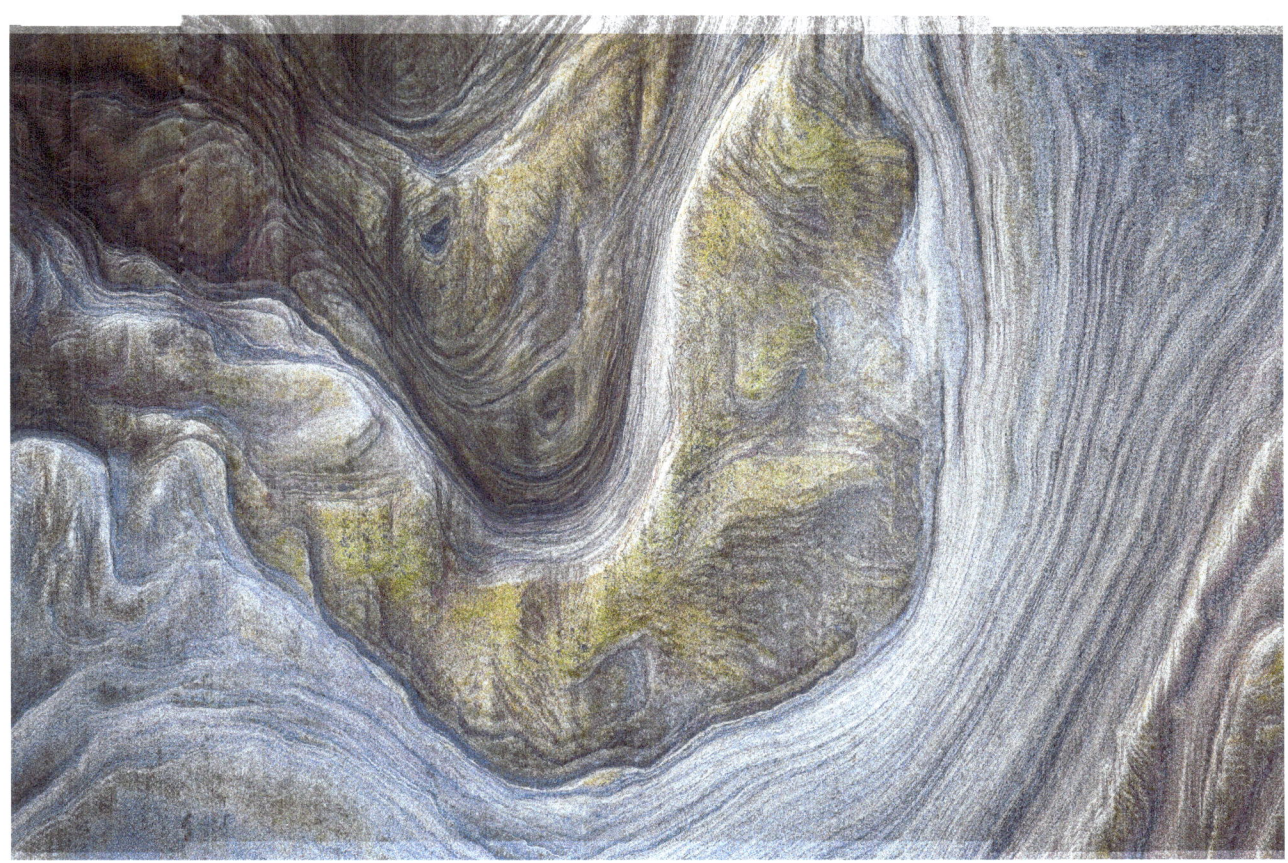

Untitled by Tom Lowe

The receding tide reveals new worlds etched in the geology of the Northumberland coast.
Canon EOS 6D, Canon EF24-105mm f/4L IS USM at 105mm, ISO100, Tripod and Circular Polariser
Judged by Amar Sood
Week 26

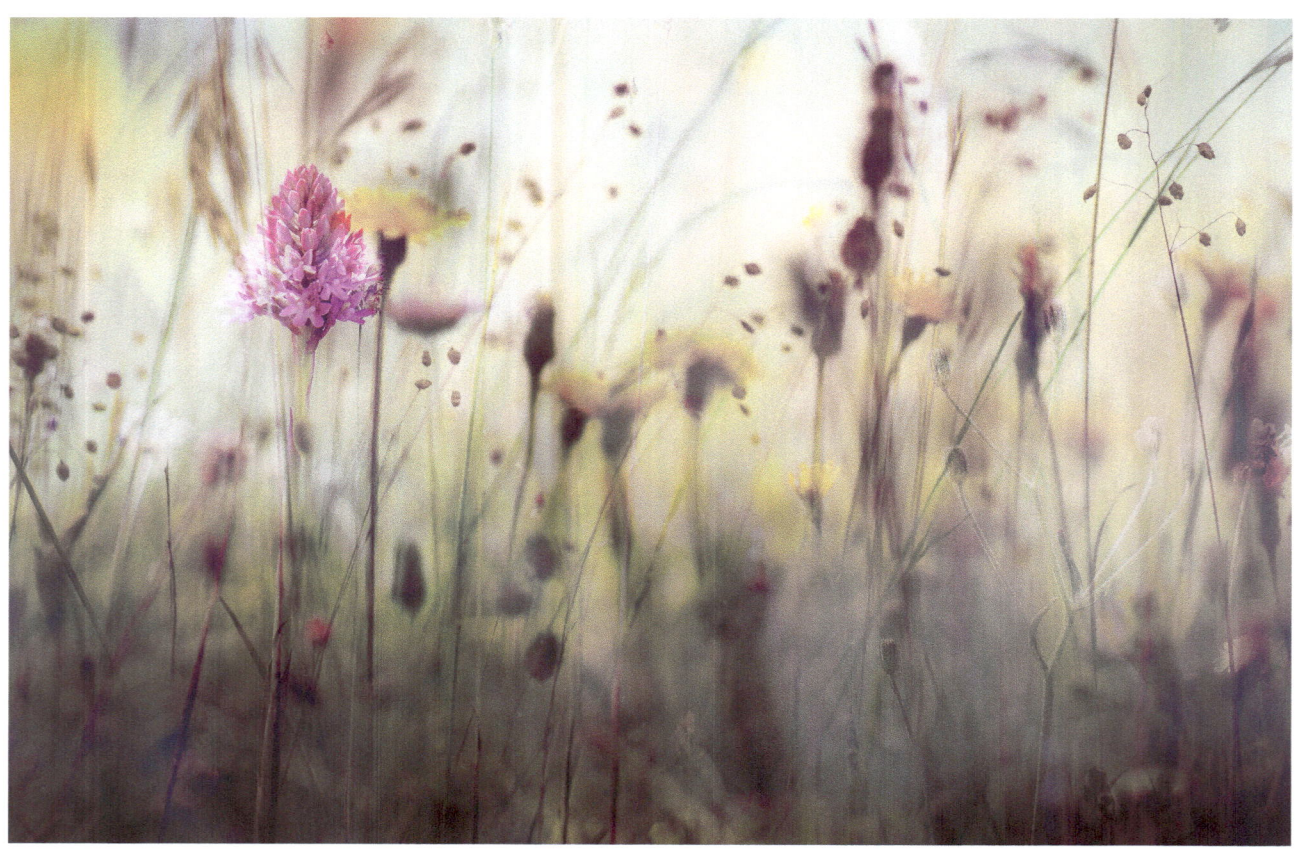

Pyramidal orchid and quaking oat grass by Jo Stephen

Sony A58 SLT Tamron 90mm f2.8 F2.8 1/4000 sec ISO 100 Handheld. No filters.
Judged by Tom Lowe
Week 27

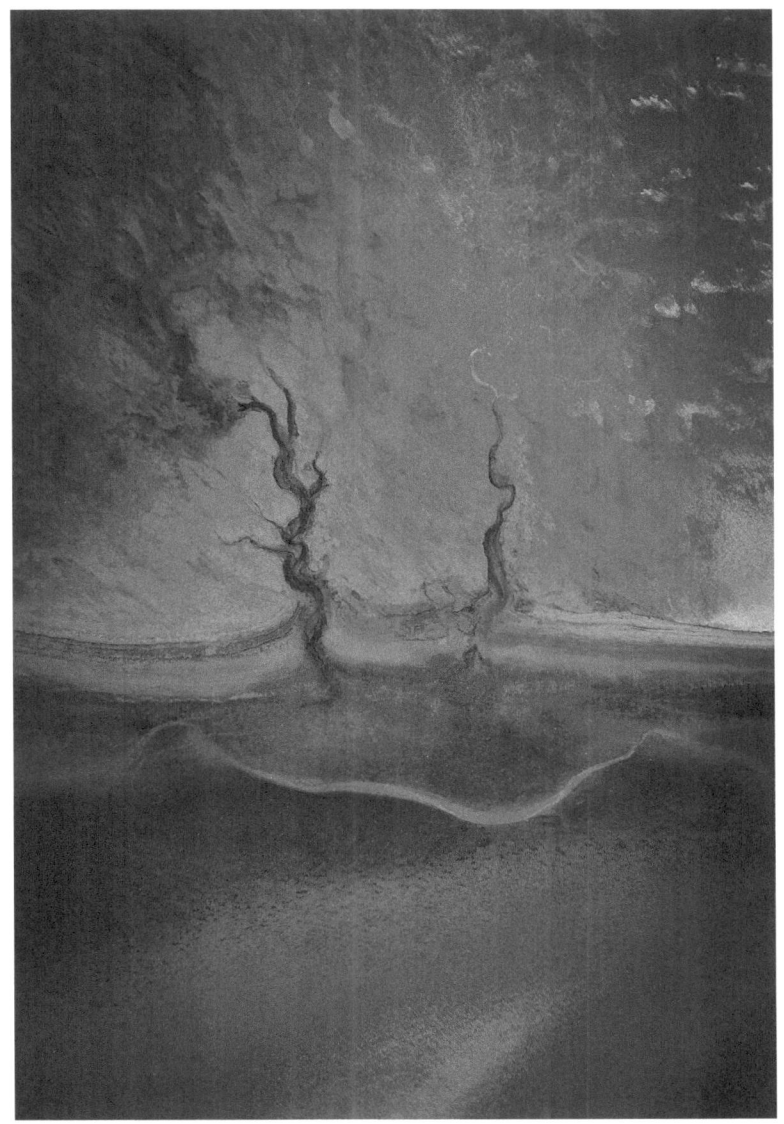

Gestalt by Neil Moran

A top down shot of sandbanks on the River Mersey at low tide. I loved the patterns of the tributaries and rivulets left behind giving off a look of trees and branches.
Mavic 2 Pro drone Iso 100 f/9.0 1/80sec
Judged by Jo Stephen
Week 28

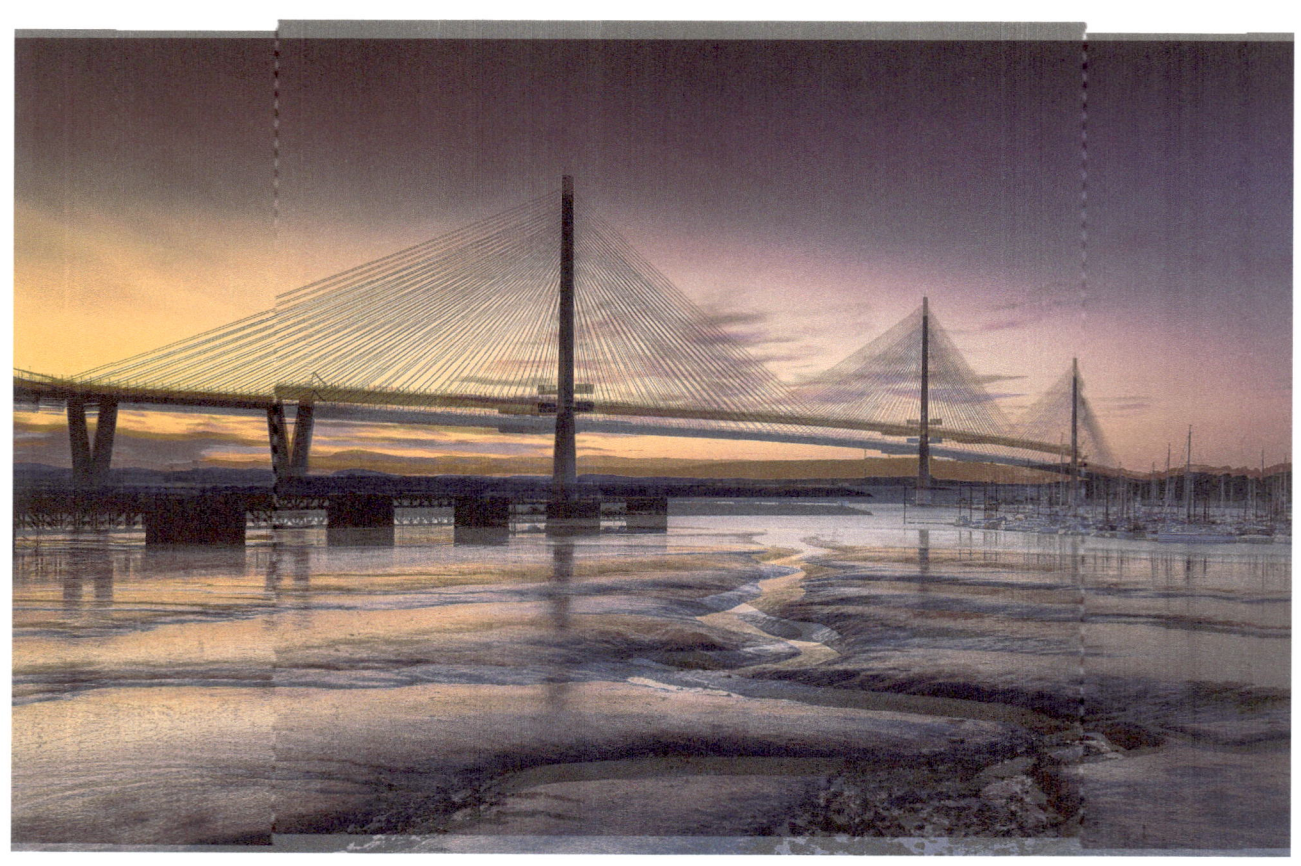

Queensferry Crossing at Sunset by Stuart Sly
Nikon D810, 16-35 @ 22mm F11 6sec ISO 100 - Lee 0.6 Soft Grad
Judged By Noel Moran
Week 29

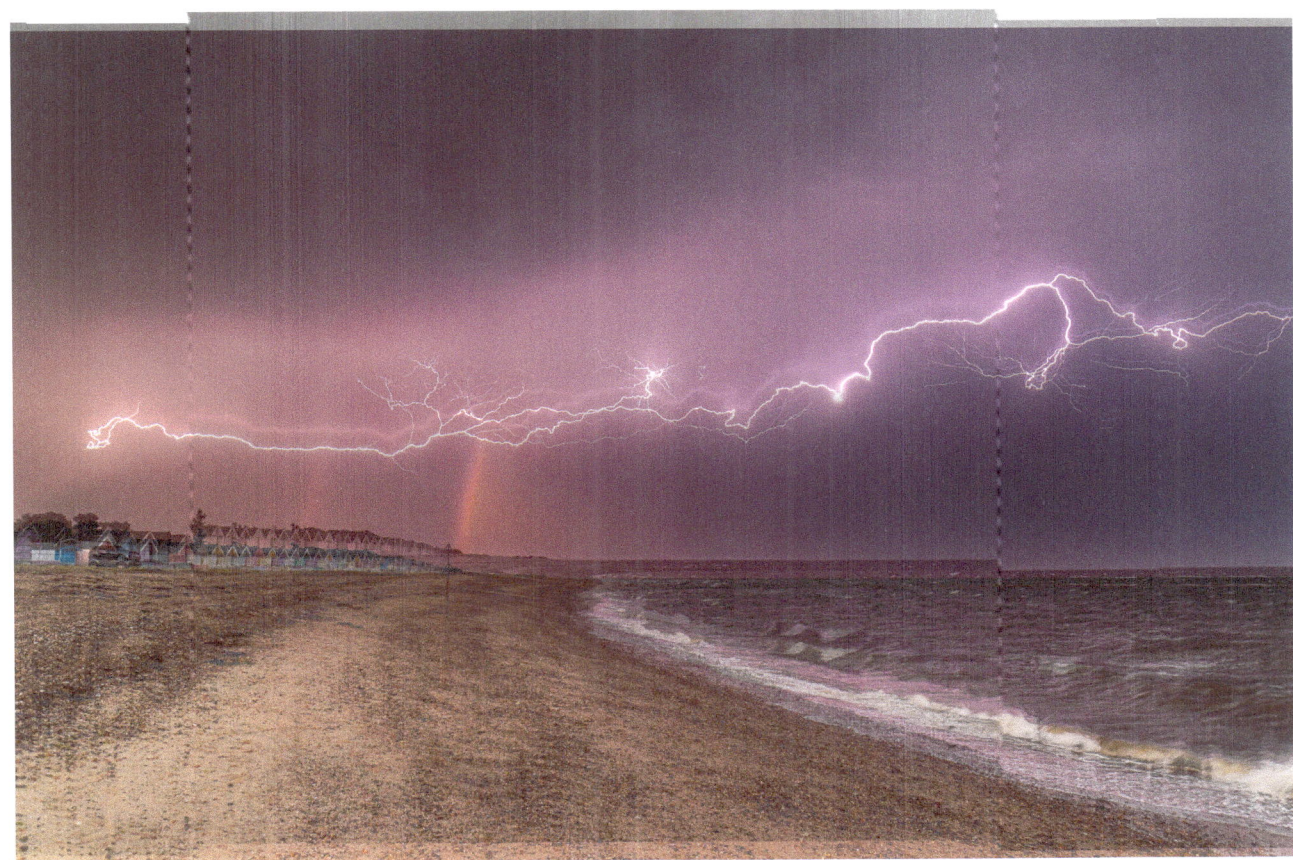

Rainbow Strike by Shaun Mills

Image was taken on Mersea Island beach at the end of a very hot, humid spell. I could see a thunder storm brewing in the distance so made a mad dash down to the beach & set up the camera on a tripod facing where I'd seen some lightning strikes in the distance. The sea was still shining brightly & in turn & one such moment a rainbow appeared. Thunder & Lightning were more regular now & I manually clicked the shutter when I could see the lightning for the 1/20th second I usually had to get lucky & captured this image.

Canon 5Dmk4, EF 24-70mm f/2.8 lens at 28mm, f/4 1/20 sec ISO 400.

Judged by Stuart Sly

Week 30

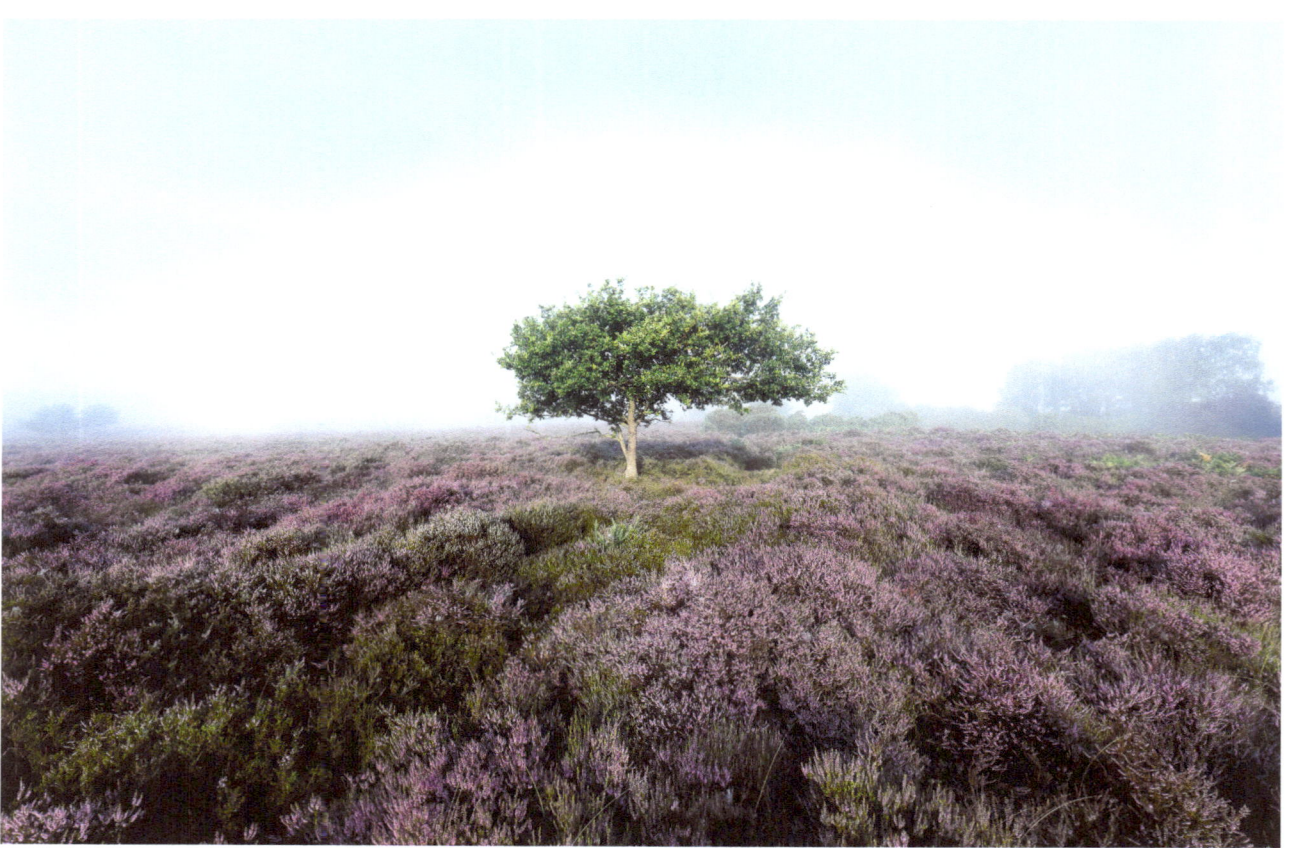

Fog bow by Martin Tosh

Out exploring Roydon Common Norfolk Wildlife Trust on a misty August morning, I was pleased as punch to see my first ever fog bow…and even more pleased to not fluff a lens change in order to get a shot of it before it disappeared! Nikon D750, Nikon 14-24 f2.8, 16mm @f11, 1/50s, ISO 100, Tripod

Judged by Shaun Mills

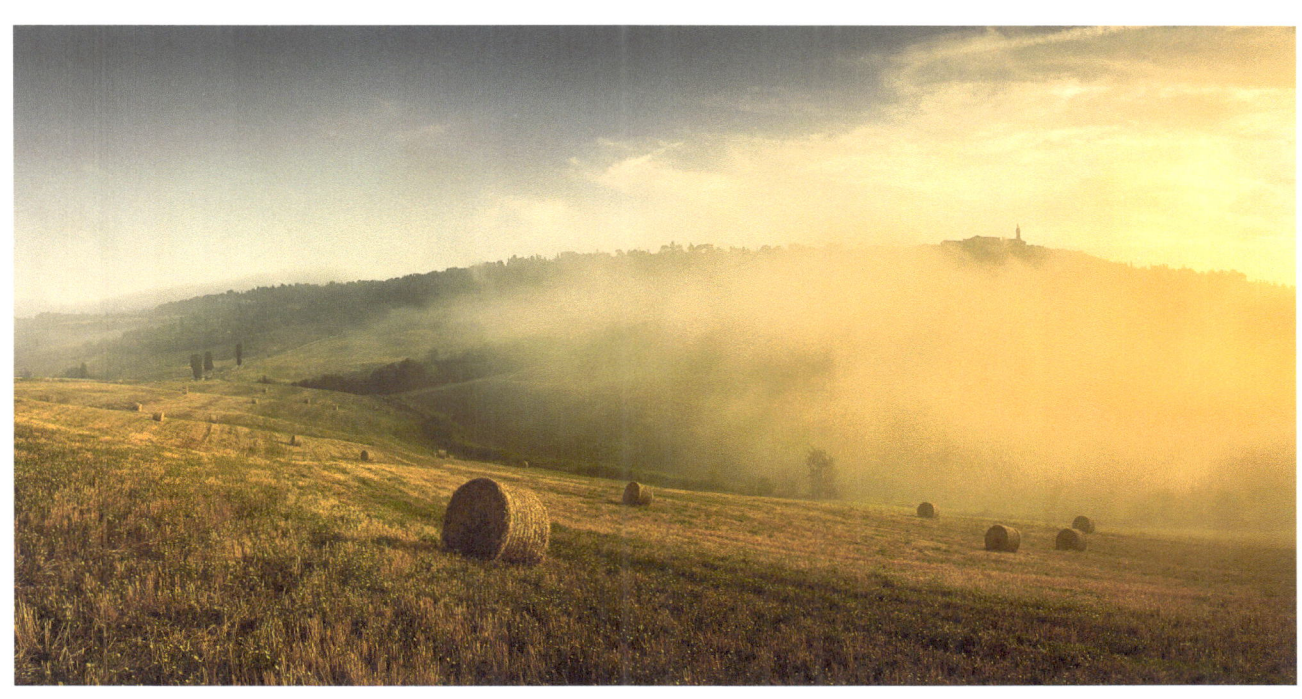

Foggy Hills by Tony Sellen

Jusdged by Martin Tosh
Week 32

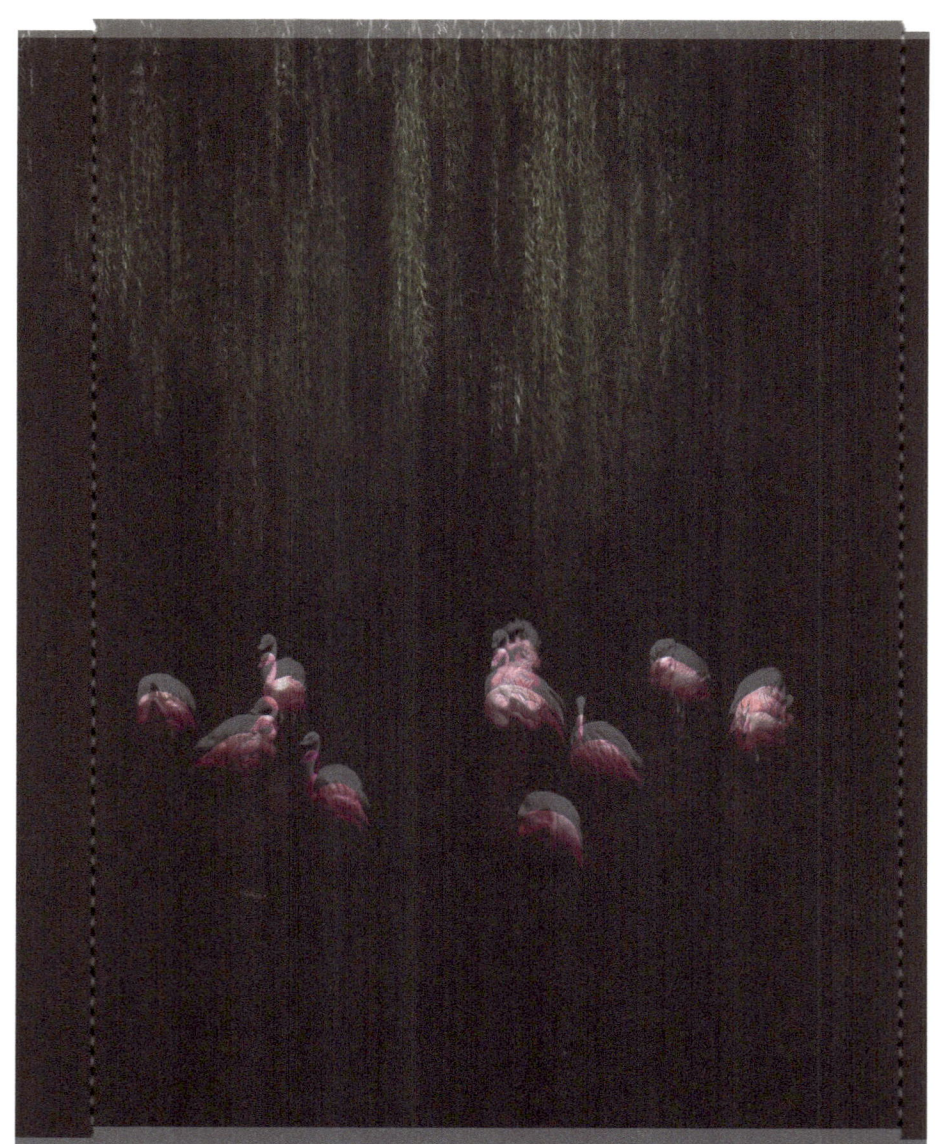

Flamingos dancing under a willow chandelier by Ashley Groom
From a exotic trip to flamingo land in Yorkshire. Sony a7iii 24-70mm f2.8 GM at 70mm 1/640 sec, @ f/2.8, iso 100.
Judged by Tony Sellen
Week 33

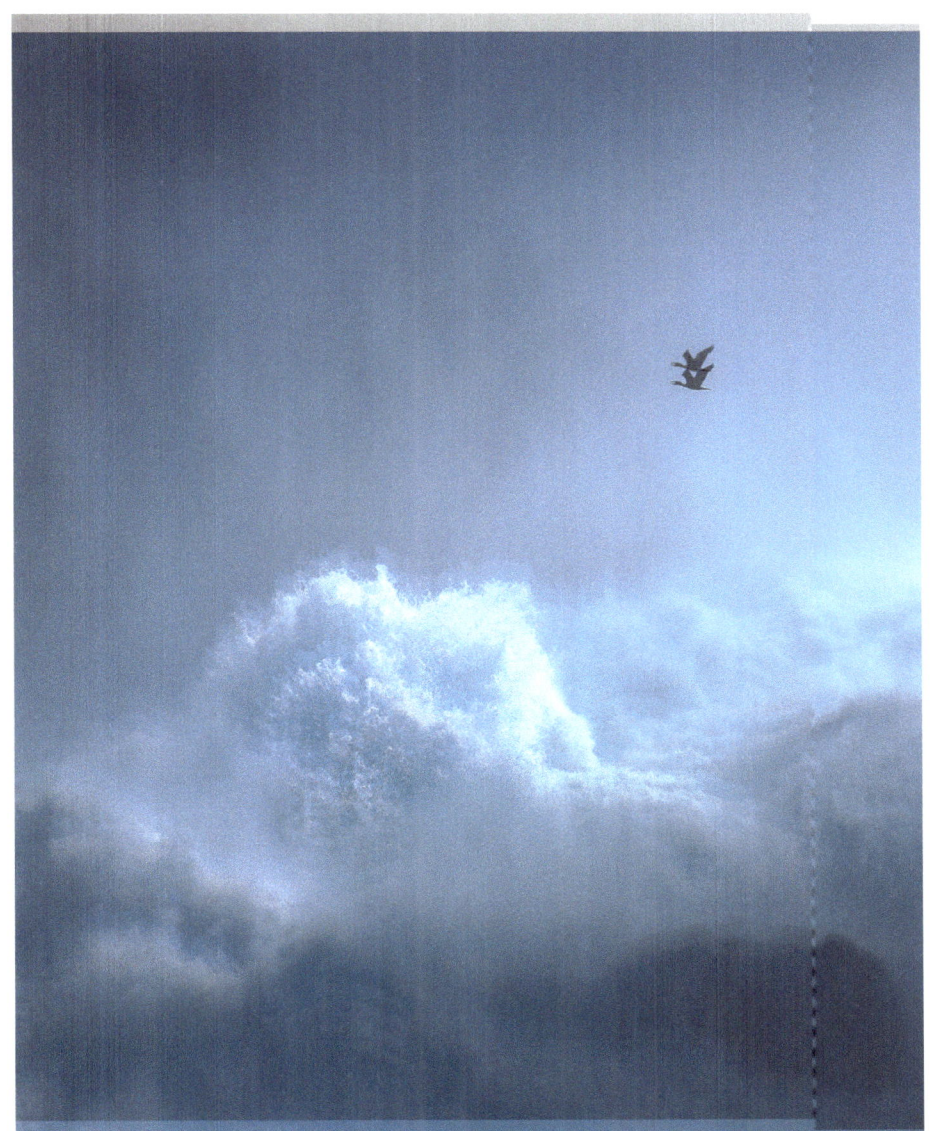

Base of the Falls by Jay Birmingham

Only having a short time in Niagara Falls, I wanted to take a different image from many of the typical ones. I wanted to capture some of the scale of the falls, but also the silhouette of the cormorants flying contrasting against the power of the falling water.

Fujifilm X-T3 with 50-230mm lens at 230mm, 1/1600 sec, f/8 at ISO 160, handheld.

Judged by Ashly Groom

Week 34

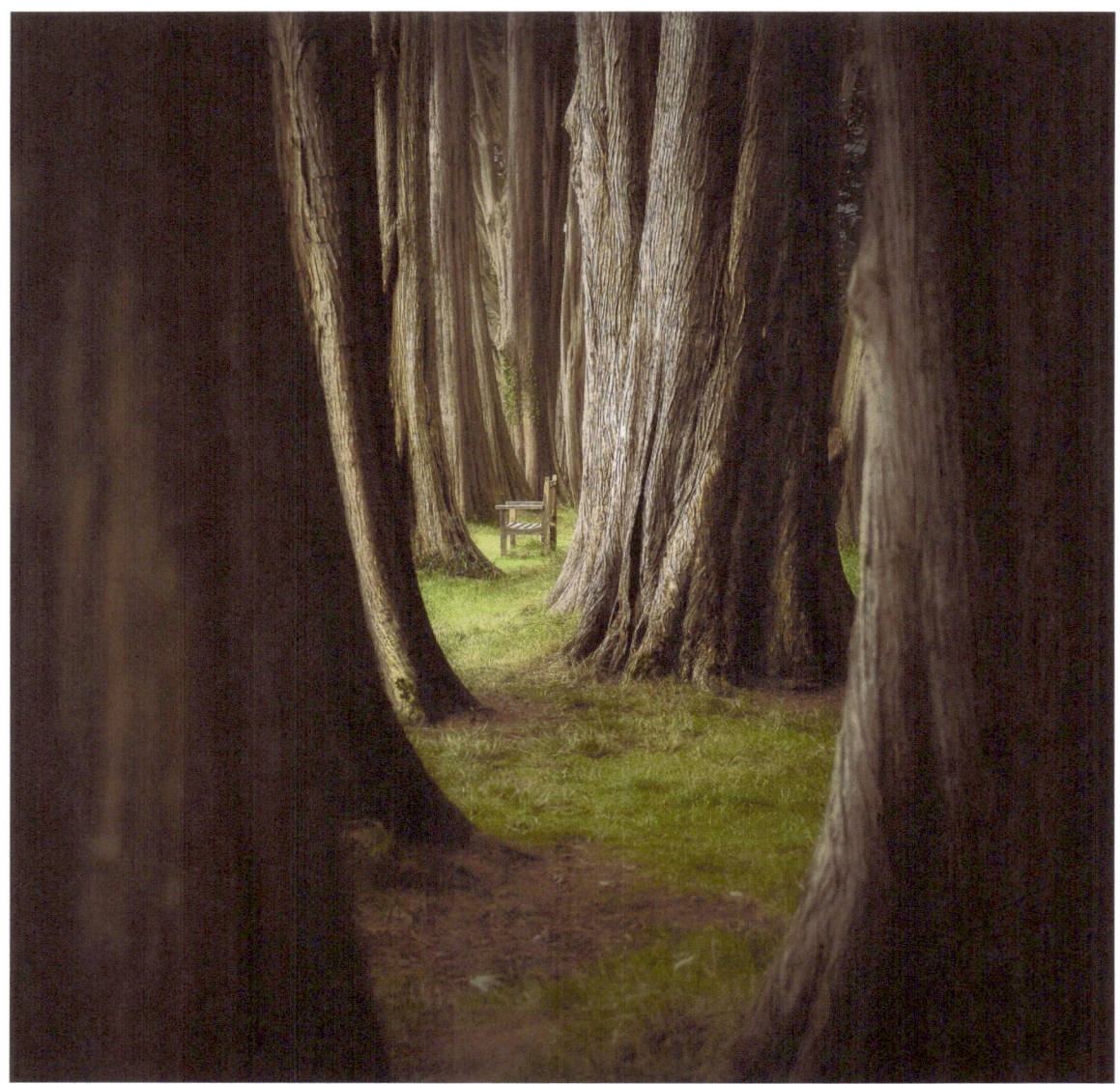

A Seat in the Woods by David Rippin

Shot on Anglesey at Plas Newydd House and Gardens. Nikon D810, Nikon 24-70mm f2.8 @ f3.5, 1/50s and ISO 500. Handheld.
Judged by Jay Birmingham
Week 35

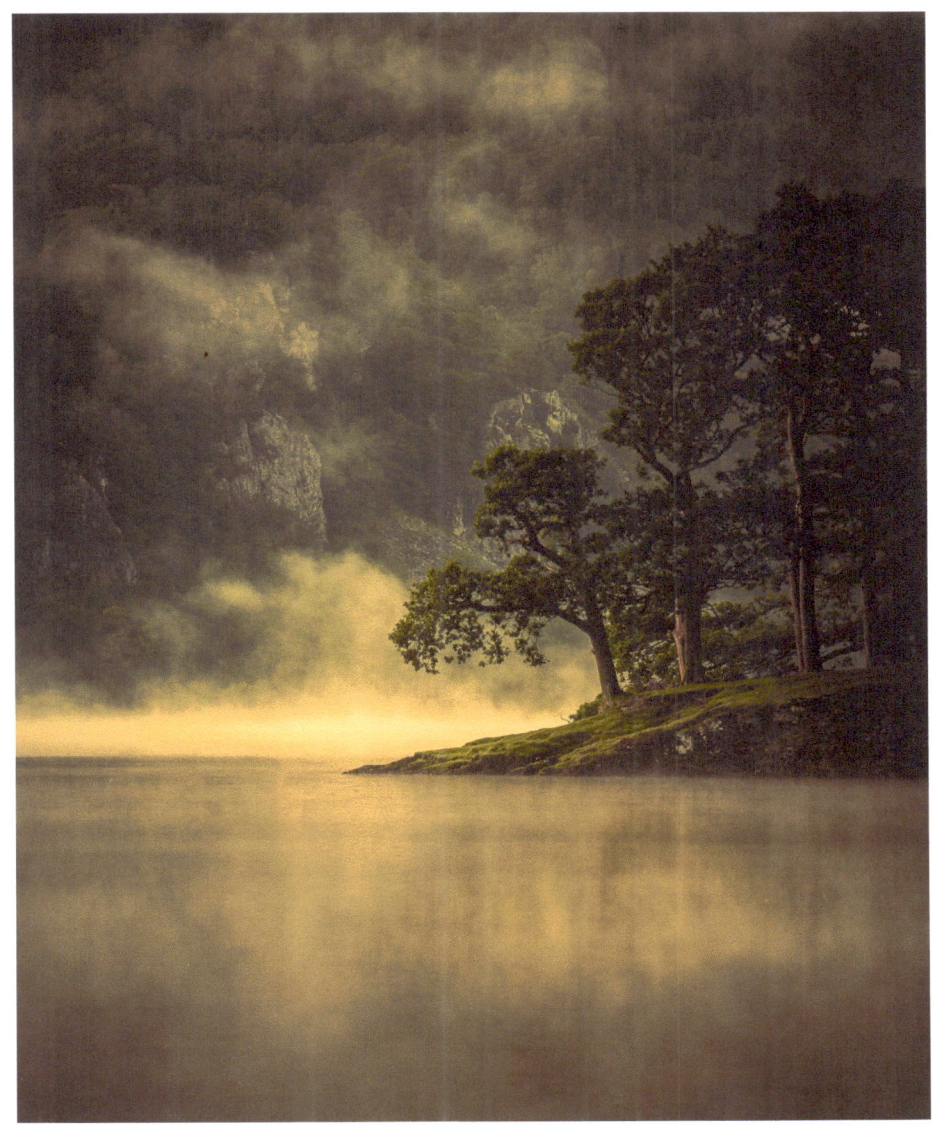

Untitled by Jason Hudson

Judged by David Rippin
Week 36

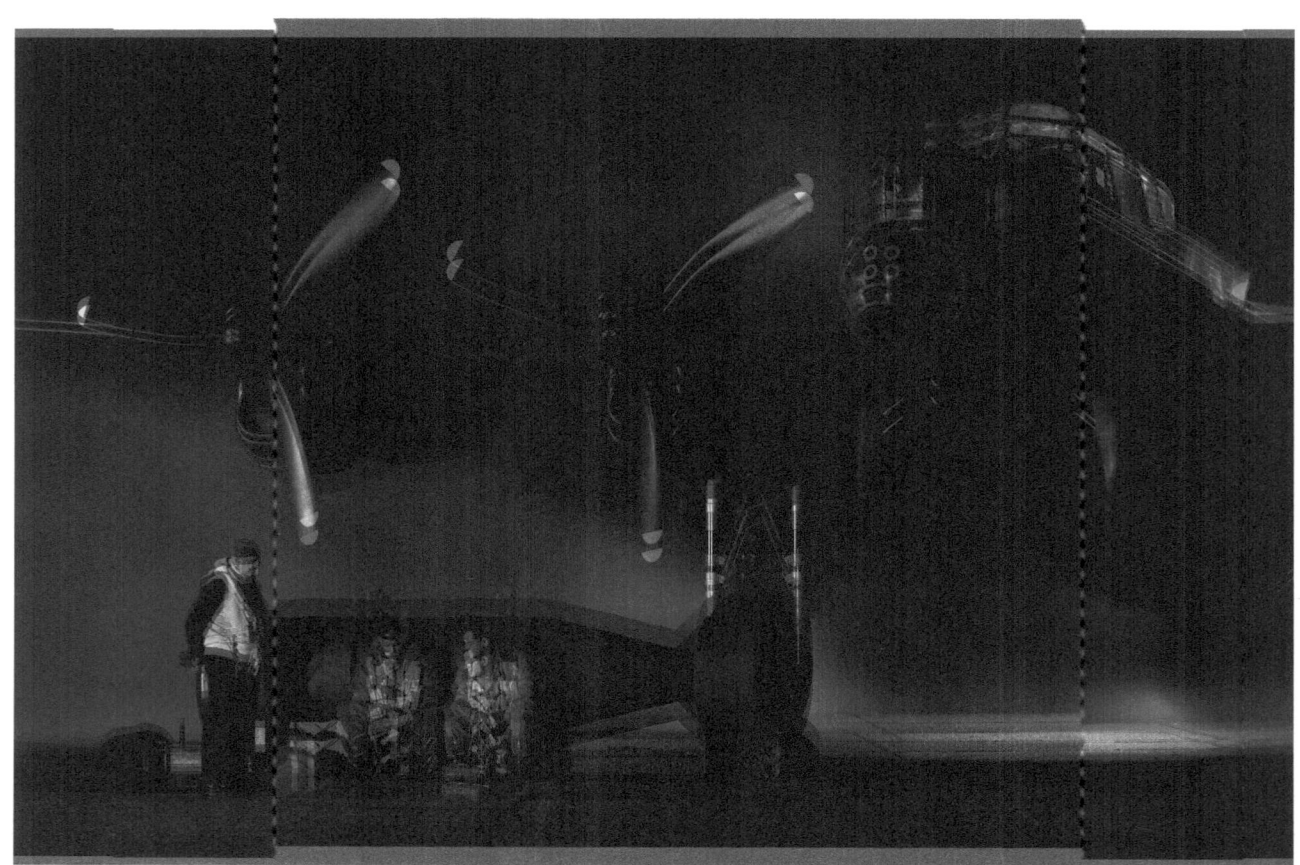

Preparing… by Alistair Jones
Just Jane with the re-enactors at the Lincolnshire Aviation Heritage Centre. Evening organised by Timeline Events.
Sony A7III, Canon EF135mmF2L (Metabones MkIV adapter) @ f7.1, 2.5 seconds and ISO 640. Tripod.
Judged By Jak Hudson
Week 37

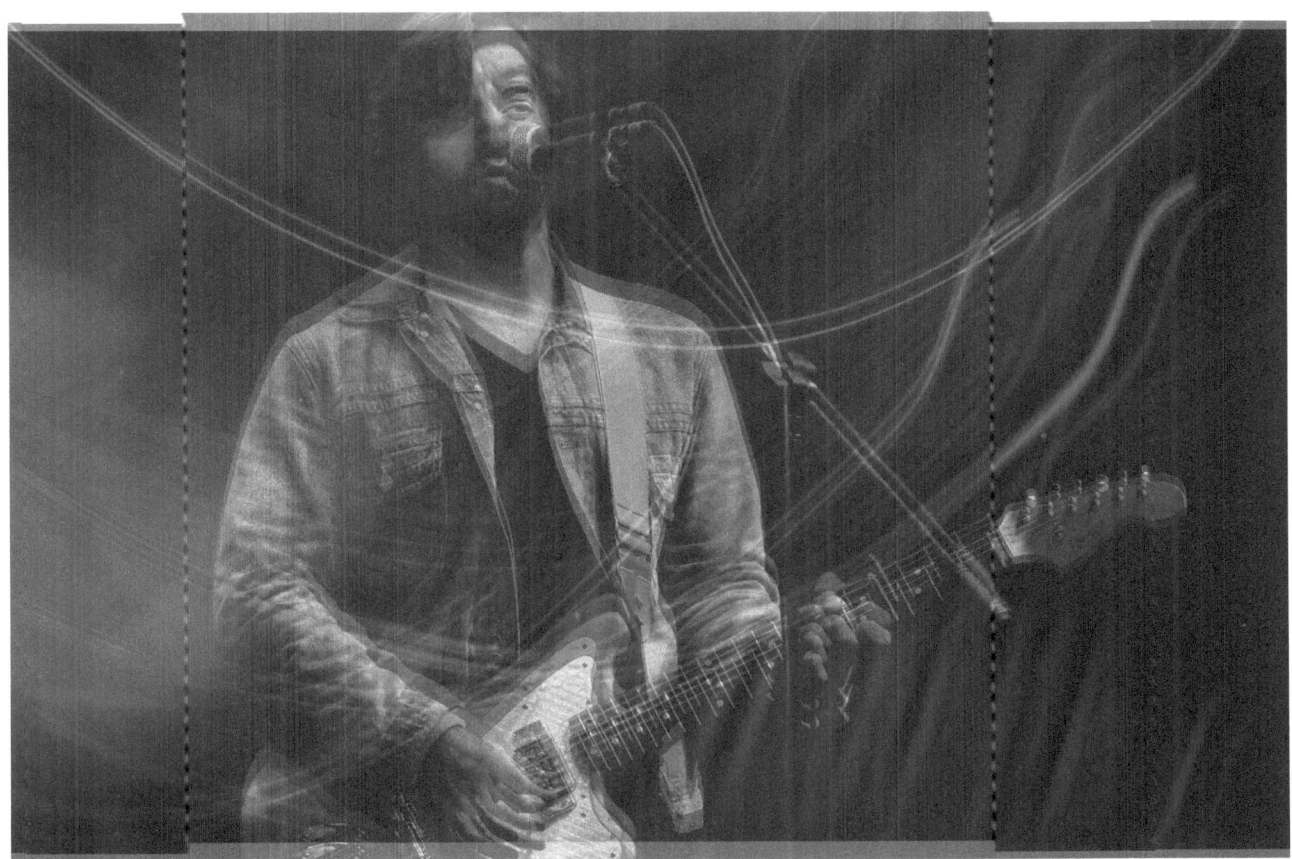

Electrify by Sarah Longes

From experiments with multiple exposures and ICM, to express the feelings and attitude of music and musicians. This image of Will Purdue was taken at the Americana Festival, held at the Fiery Bird in Woking. It's a double exposure with the second being a long exposure with movement. The equivalent exposure would be about 1/60 f6.5 ISO 1000. FUJIFILM X-T2 Double exposure with Fujifilm 100-400mm at 115mm and 400mm, 173mm and 600mm equivalent. 2 sec. Made up of 1/60 f6.8 and 1/60 f4.6 ISO 4000

Judged by Alistair Jones

Week 38

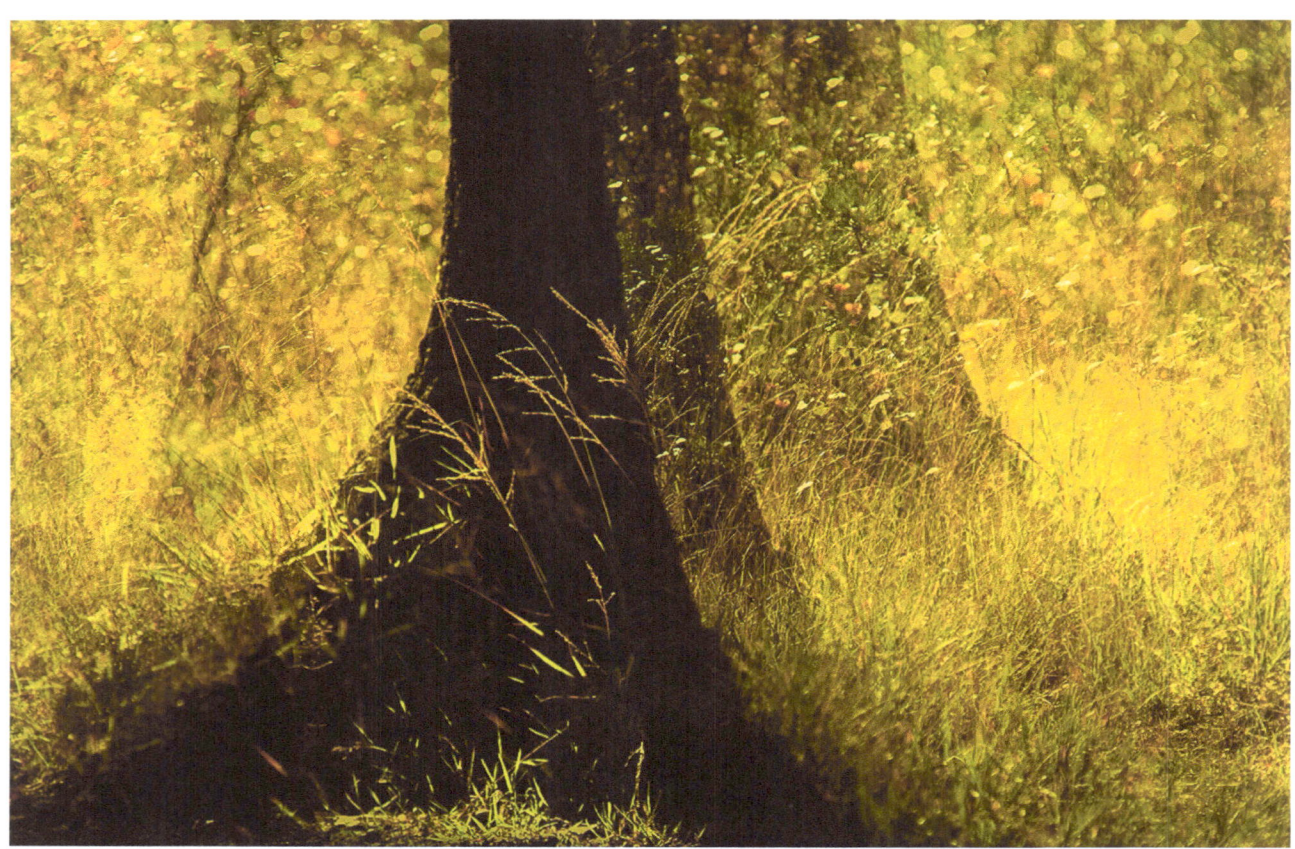

Stedham Common by Elke Epp

Taken on 28.09.2019 The light was intense this Saturday morning on the Common. I decided to have a play with some multiple exposures which brought out the golden glow even more. Canon 7D II ,1/500 sec, F4, ISO800, 98mm, EF 24-105mm F4L, IS USM, Multiple Exposure of 3 images.

Judged by Sarah Longes

Week 39

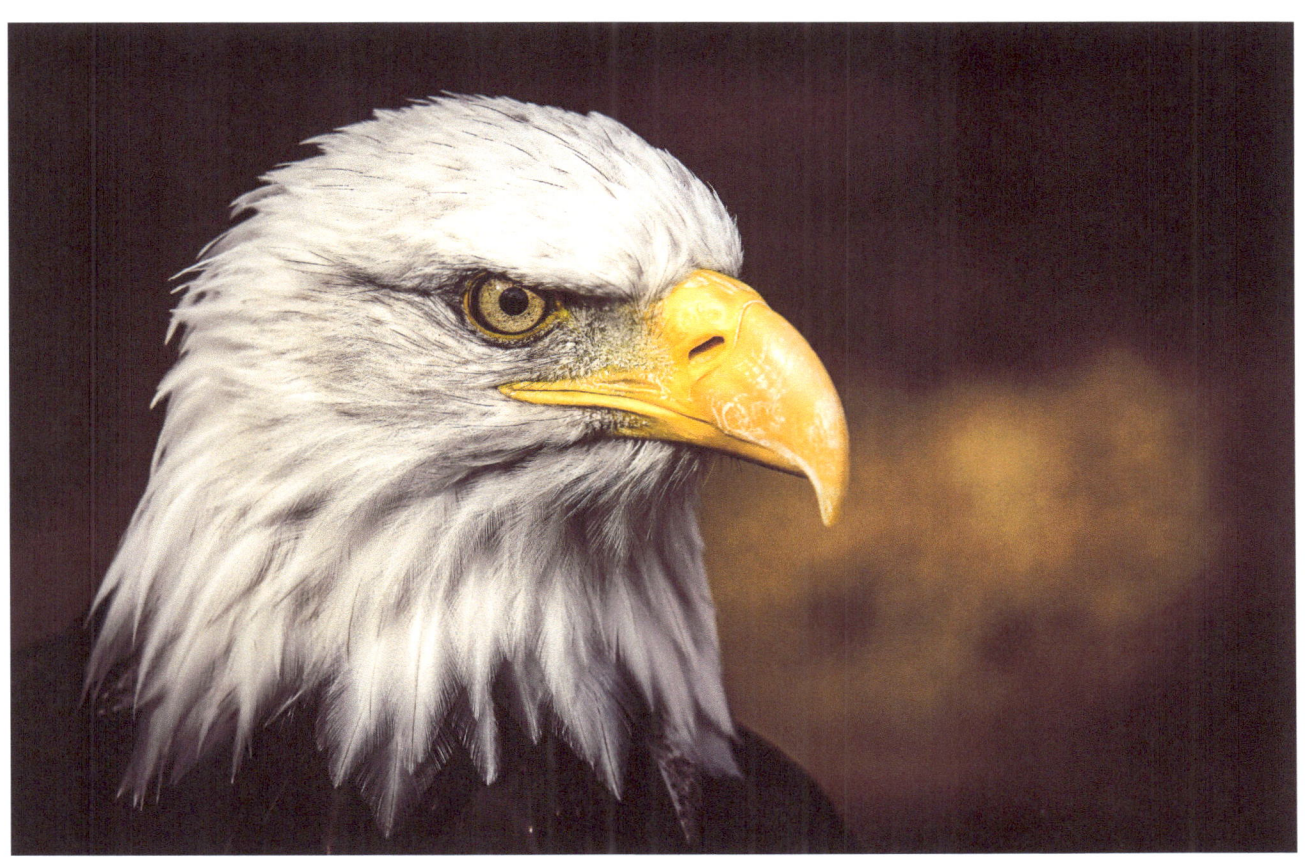

Banham Zoo's Bald Eagle by Simon Watling

Taken on a sony a77ii with my trusty old heavy sigma 100-300 f4 lens. $f/4.0$ 180.0 mm   1/1250   iso100

Judged by Elke Epp

Week 40

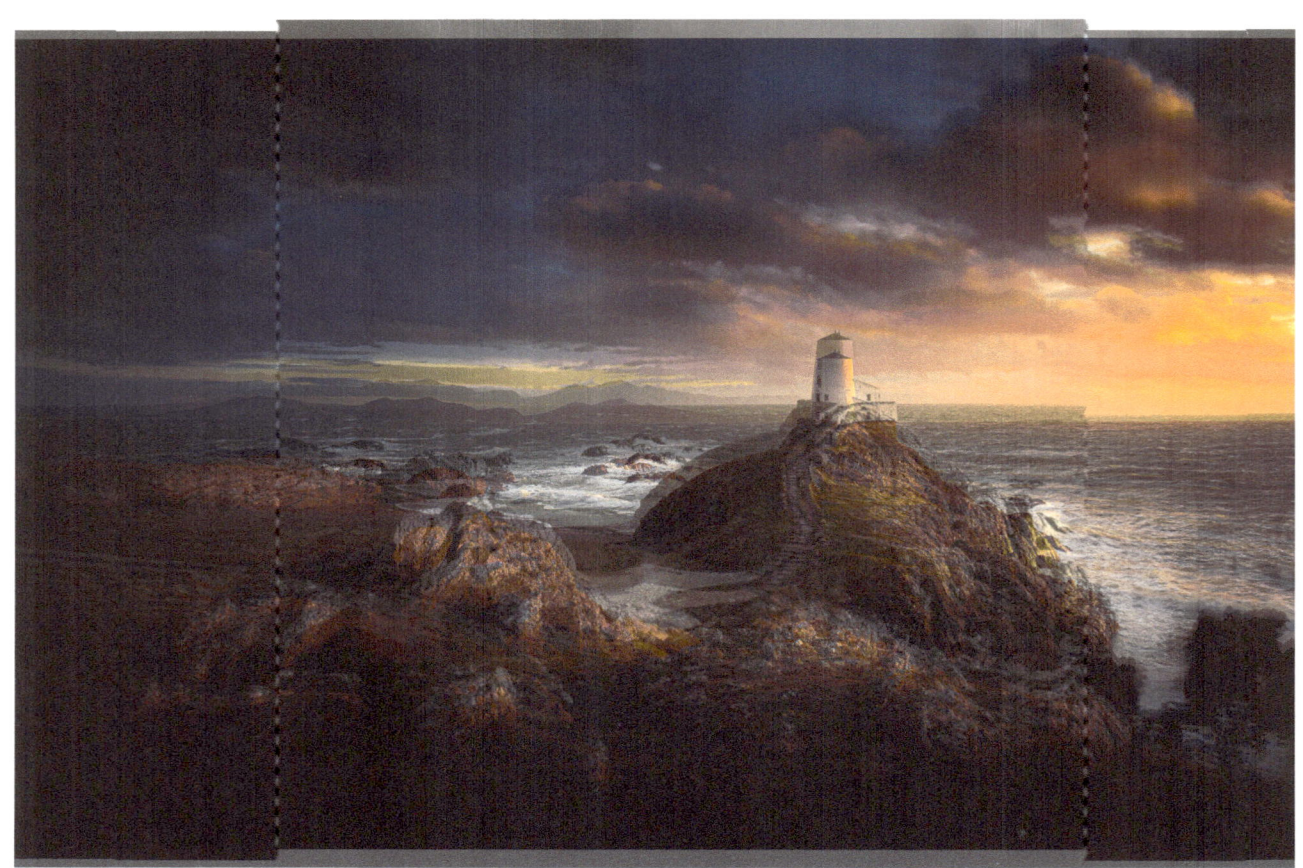

Distant Three by Gareth Mon James
Llanddwyn Island as a weather front passes just in time for a lovely sunset
my favorite image from this location Nikon D850 Nikon 24-70mm f2.8 f/9 iso 80 1/4 sec kase 4stop soft grad
Judged by Simon Waitling
Week 41

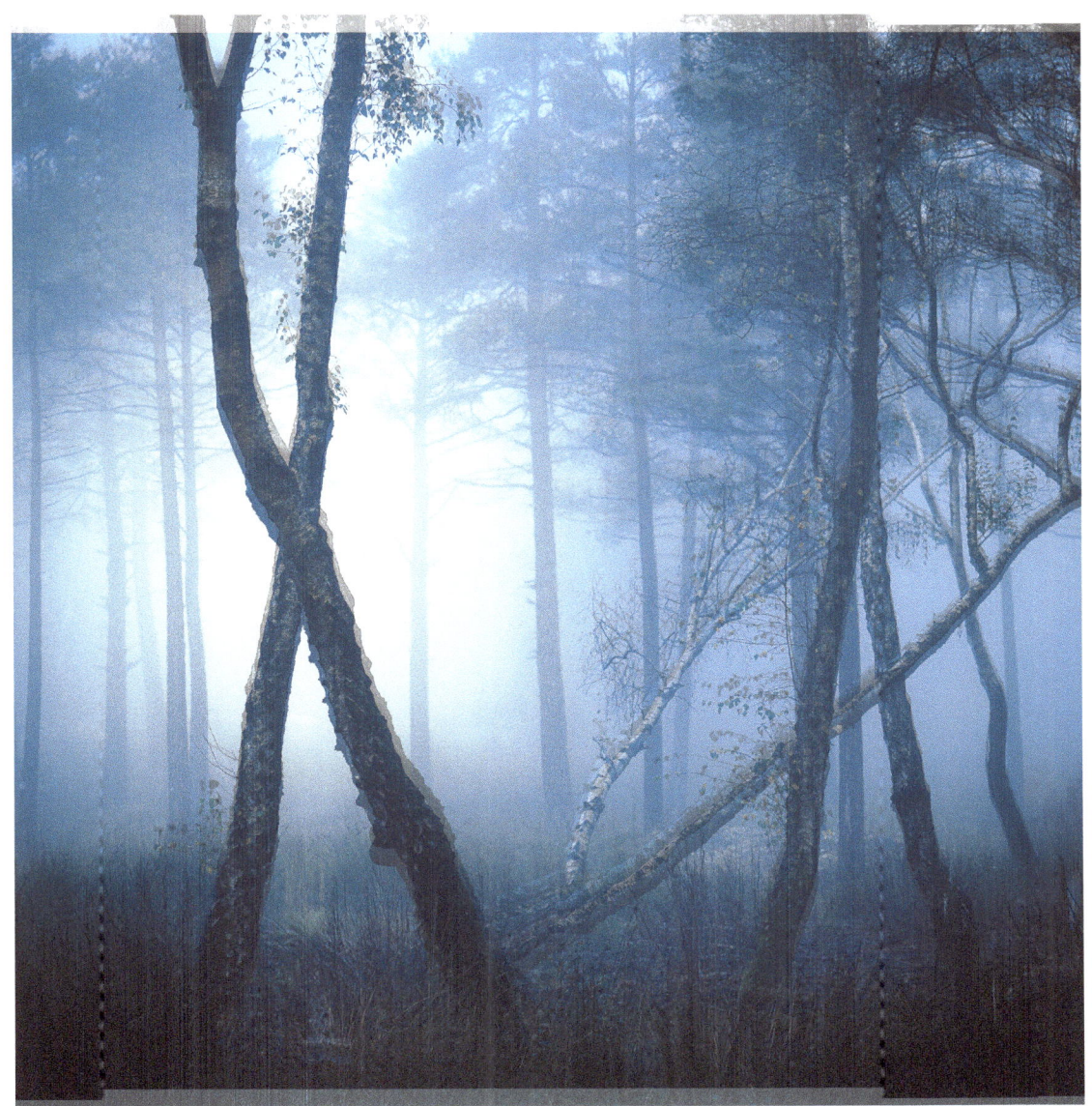

Crossover by Andy Luddington
Canon EOS 70D Canon EF 70-200mm L USM f/4 1/80 sec ISO 100 70mm No flash or filters Processed in Lr and Ps
Judged by Ken Mon Jones
Week 42

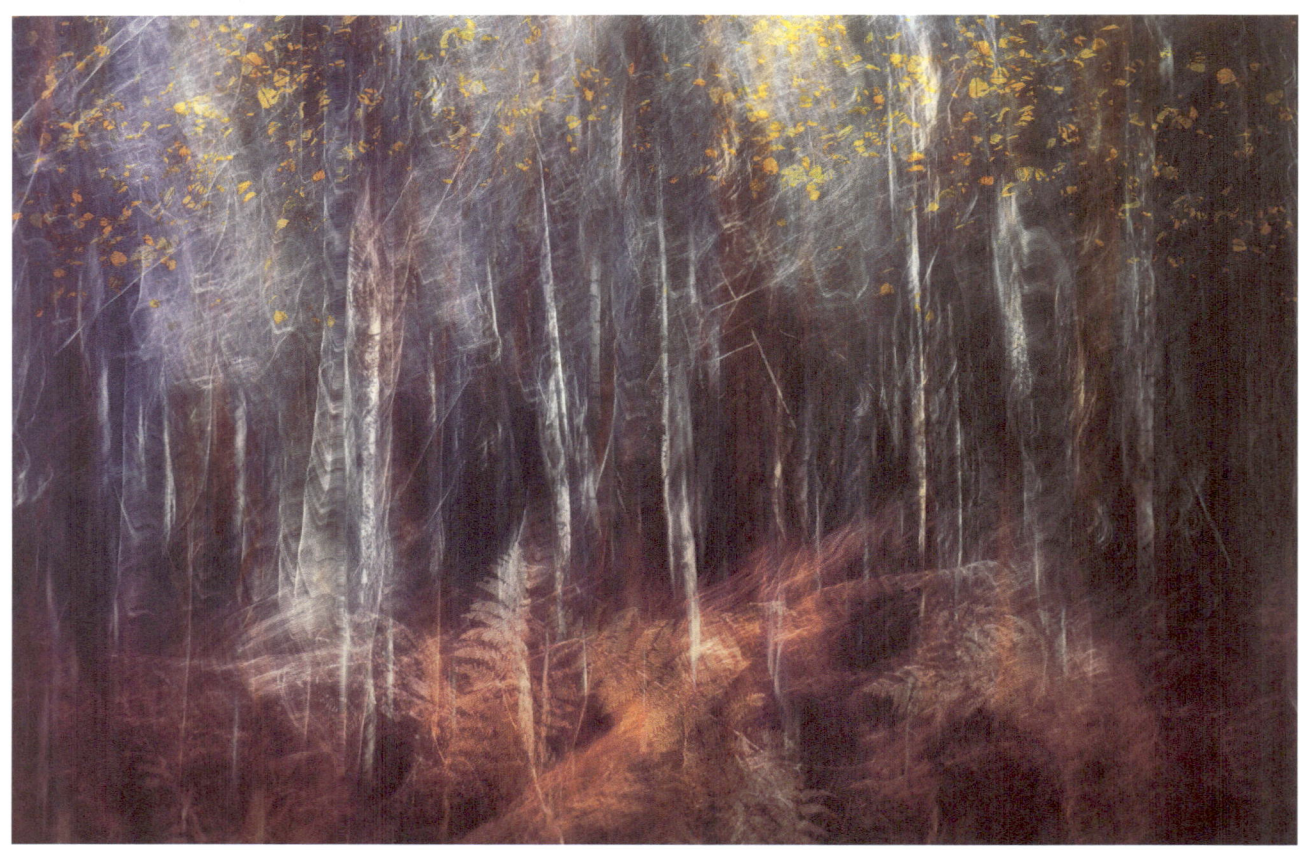

Arne by Jo Stephen

Sony A58 SLT Tamron 90mm f2.8 F13 ISO 100 ¼ sec Handheld. No filter.
Judged by Andy Luddington
Week 43

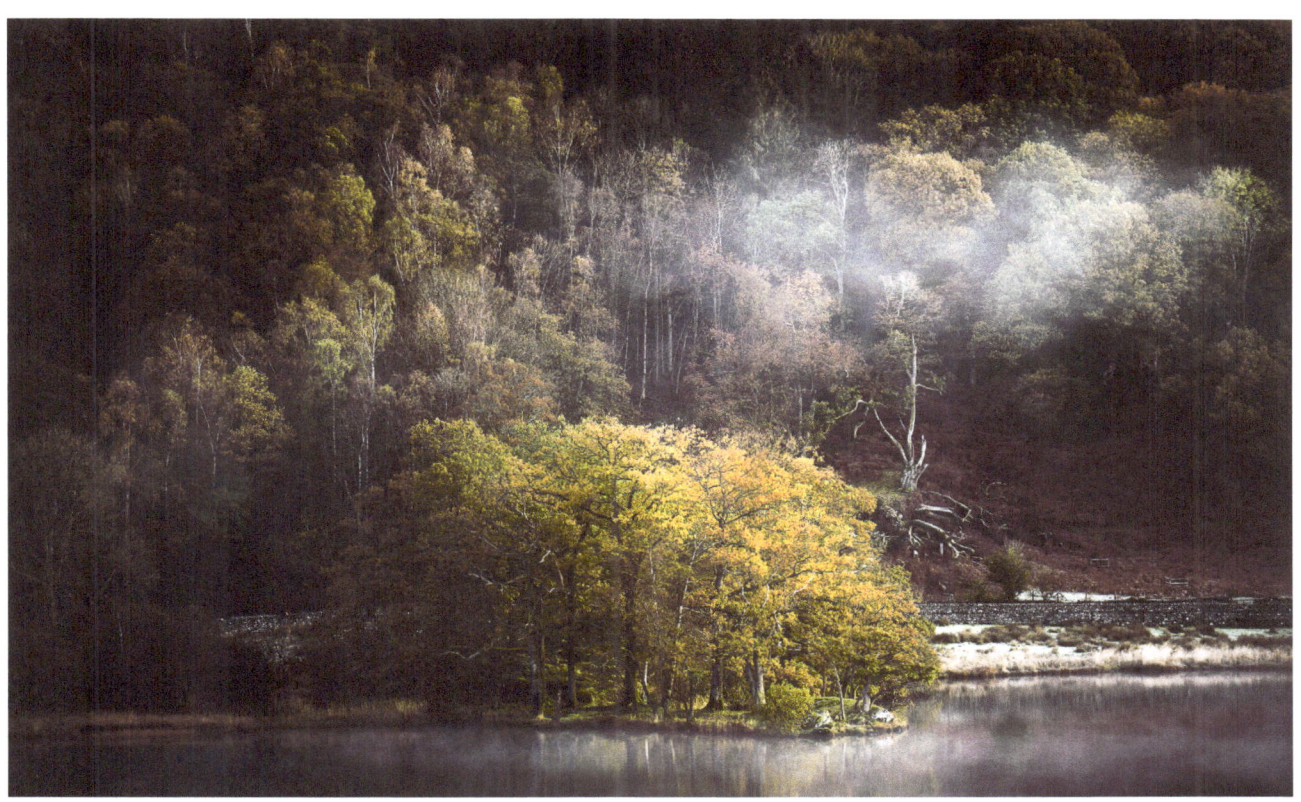

Rydal Water by Amar Sood

This was not the image I had set out to take on the day. There was heavy mist in the forecast and I was staying in Keswick. I knew Derwentwater would be crawling with photographers so I decided to head to Rydal Water in the hope that it would be quieter. On arriving I went for a walk around the lake and spotted little wispy bits of mist forming on the surface of the water and then floating off into the air. I watched this for some time, getting a feel for their behaviour before I started taking photographs. This was my favourite image of the morning. I liked how the mist arches over the group of trees which were catching the light in just the right way to accentuate their autumnal colours.

Nikon Z7, Nikon 70-300mm f/4.5-5.6E ED VR AF-P @ 130mm and f/5.6, 1/60s and ISO 800. Handheld

Judged by Jo Stephen

Week 44

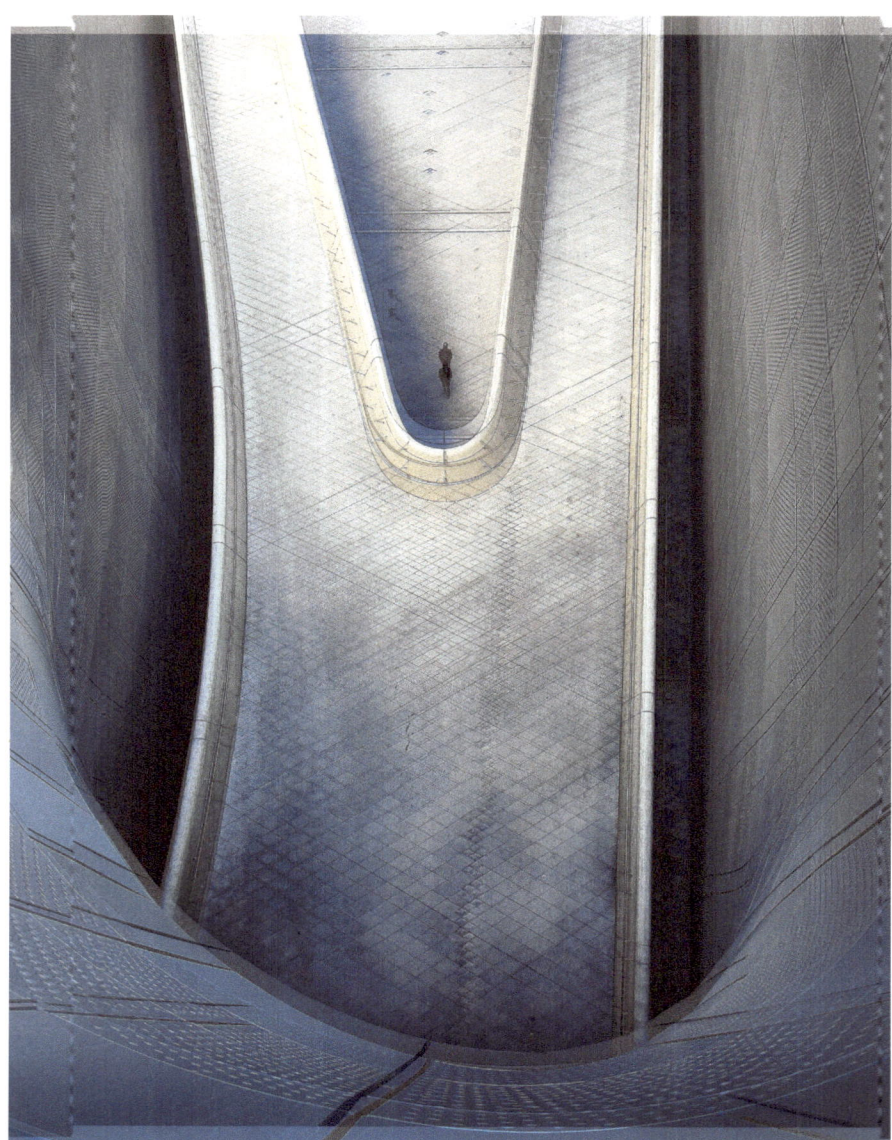

Between the Curves by Dan Portch
Dongdaemun Design Plaza, Seoul, South Korea
A hand-held mobile phone shot taken from the rooftop walkway of the futuristic design plaza building by Zaha Hadid Architects.
Mobile Phone (Samsung Galaxy Note 4) 4.8mm f/2.2 1/140 sec ISO 50
Judged by Amar Sood
Week 45

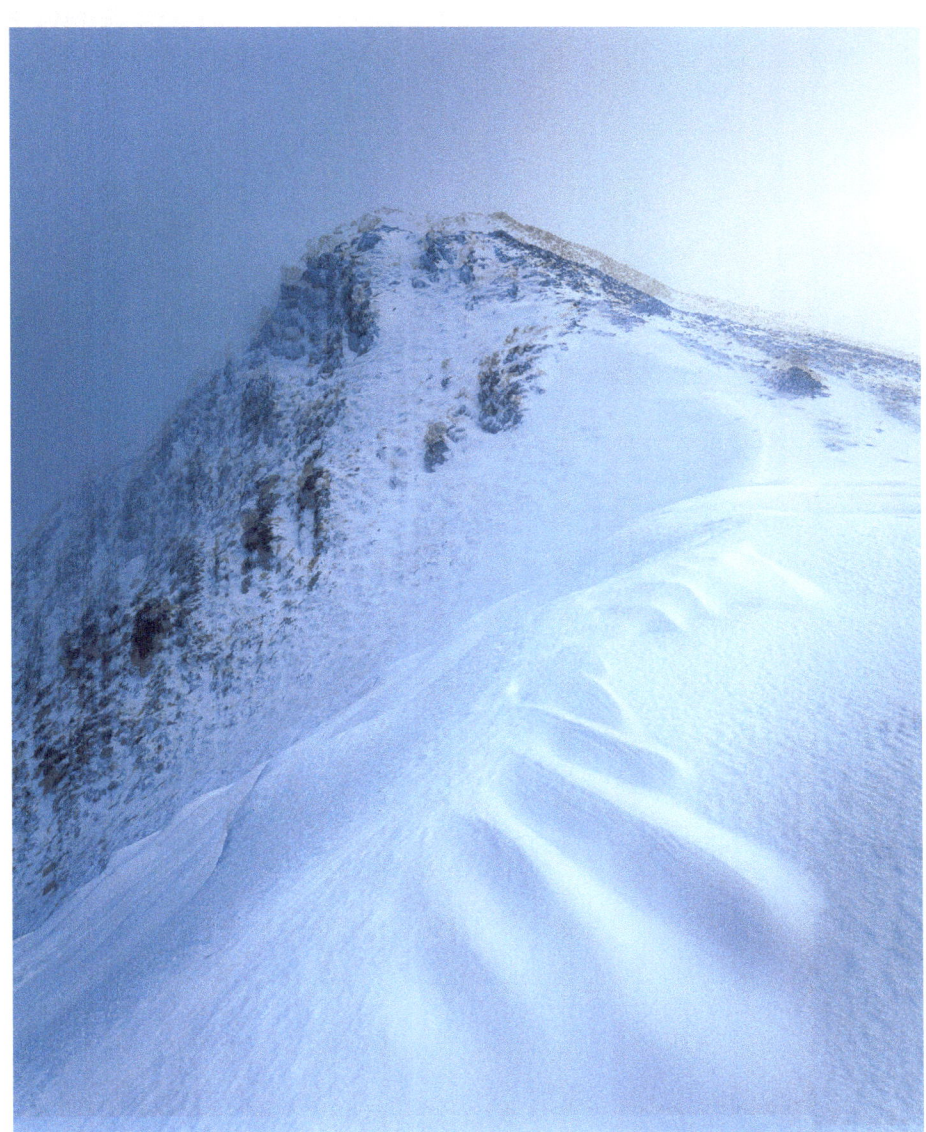

Y Garn by Ollie Pocock

An awesome afternoon heading up to Y Garn via Llyn Clyd. As I topped out on the ridge line, the wind became ferocious. I knew some of the good climbing up to Y Garn via the Llyd Ad line, this being nice to line the Canon 5D Mk IV Canon. This foreground however was too good to miss. I managed to take a few handheld shots, this being my favourite. Canon 5D MkIV, Canon 24-70mm f/L @ f10, 1/250sec ISO 100 handheld.

Judged by Dale Portch

Week 46

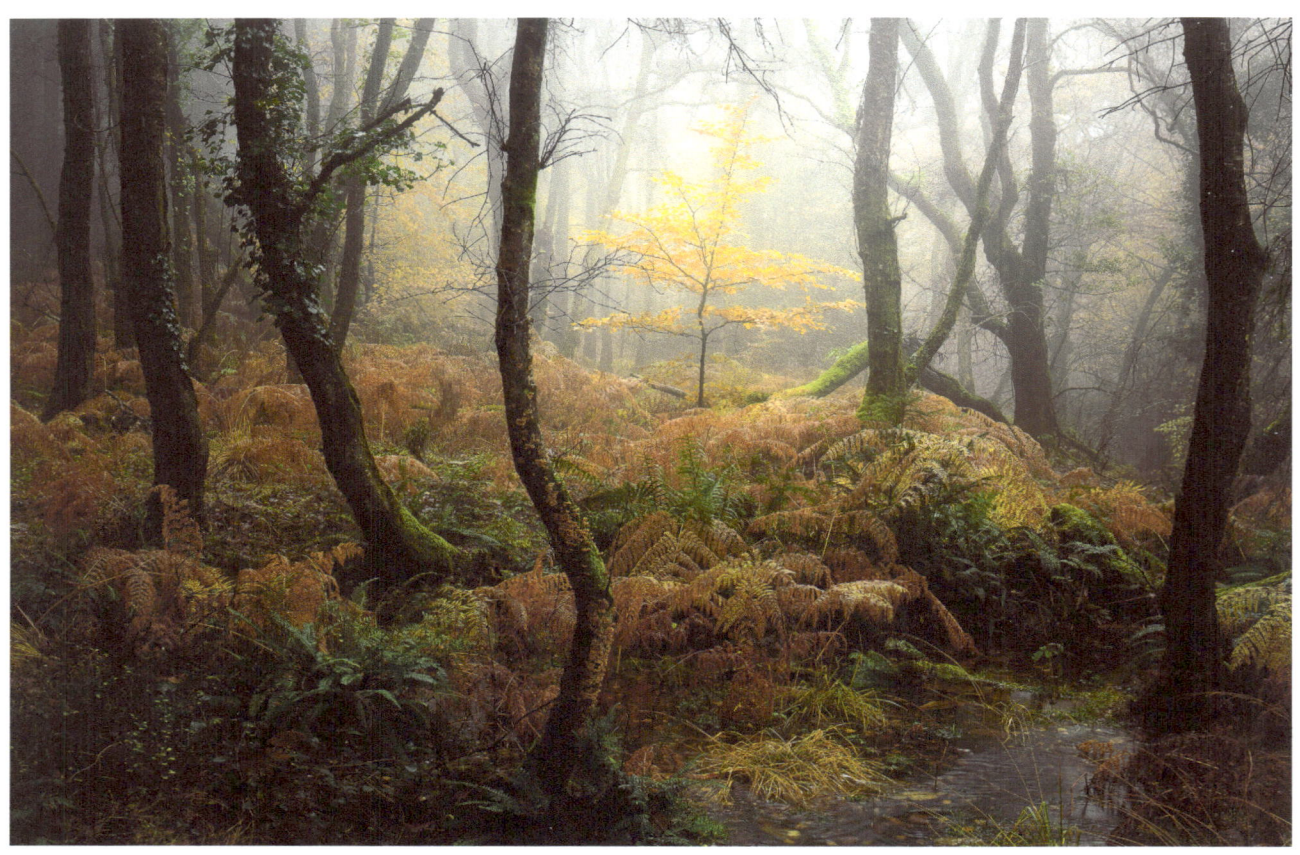

Untitled by Neil Burnell

Judged by Ollie Pocock
Week 47

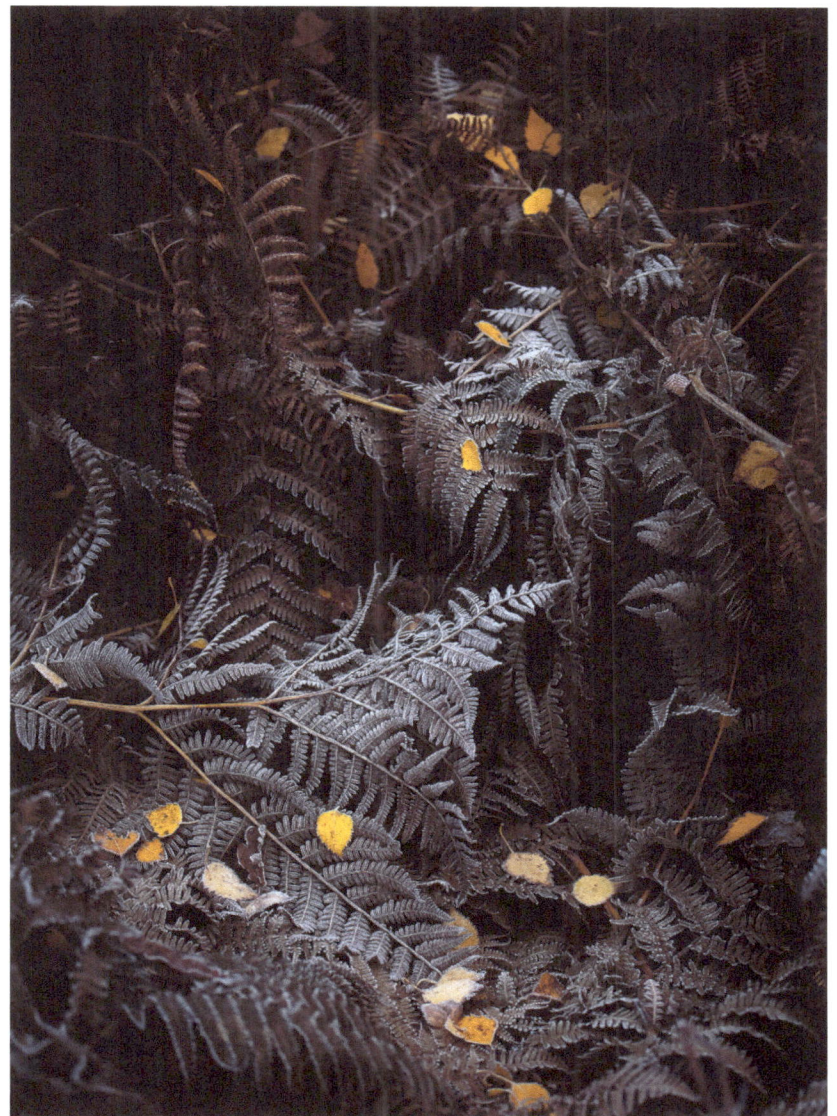

Frostilicious by Chaitanya Deshpande

I took this image late in November when Autumn had just started showing signs of giving way to Winter. The change of seasons always provides interesting opportunities for photos, and on the morning I took this image, the mix of reds, oranges and yellows from Autumns intermingled perfectly with the frosty whites of winter.
Canon 5Ds Canon EF 70-200mm f/4 L IS USM @ 70mm, f/4.0, 1/40s, ISO 500 Handheld
Judged by Neil Burnell
Week 48

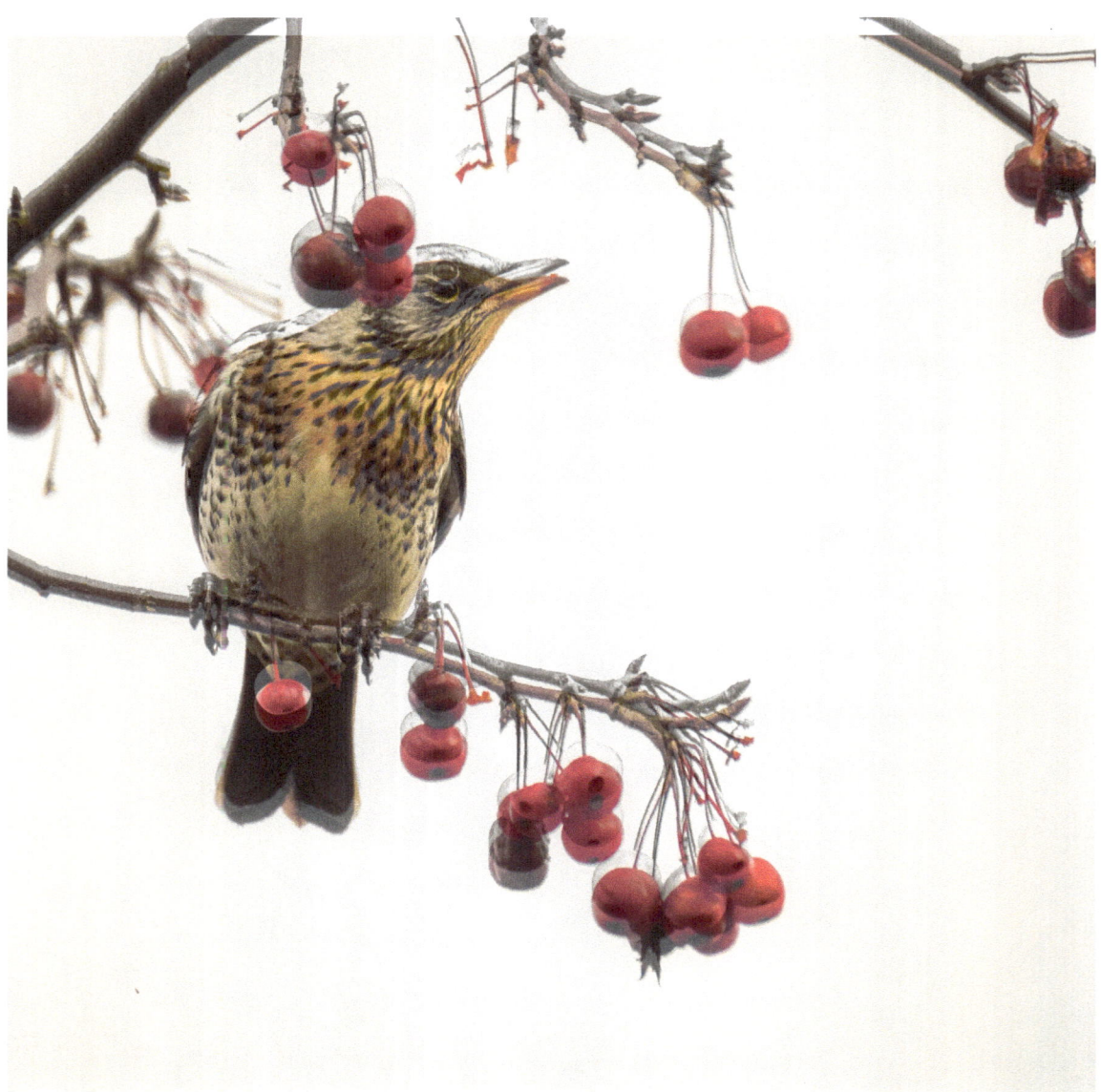

Winter Tree Decorations by Sarah Longes

This is one of my favourite tree decorations, at RHS Wisley Gardens, the fieldfare! They are members of the Thrush family that fly south from Scandinavia to overwinter in the UK and other parts of southern Europe. They come to take advantage of the berry crops here. Fujifilm X-T2 with Fujifilm XF 100-400mm and 1.4x teleconverter at 560mm; equivalent 840mm, f/8, 1/200s, ISO 2500.

Judged by Chinmay Desphande

Week 49

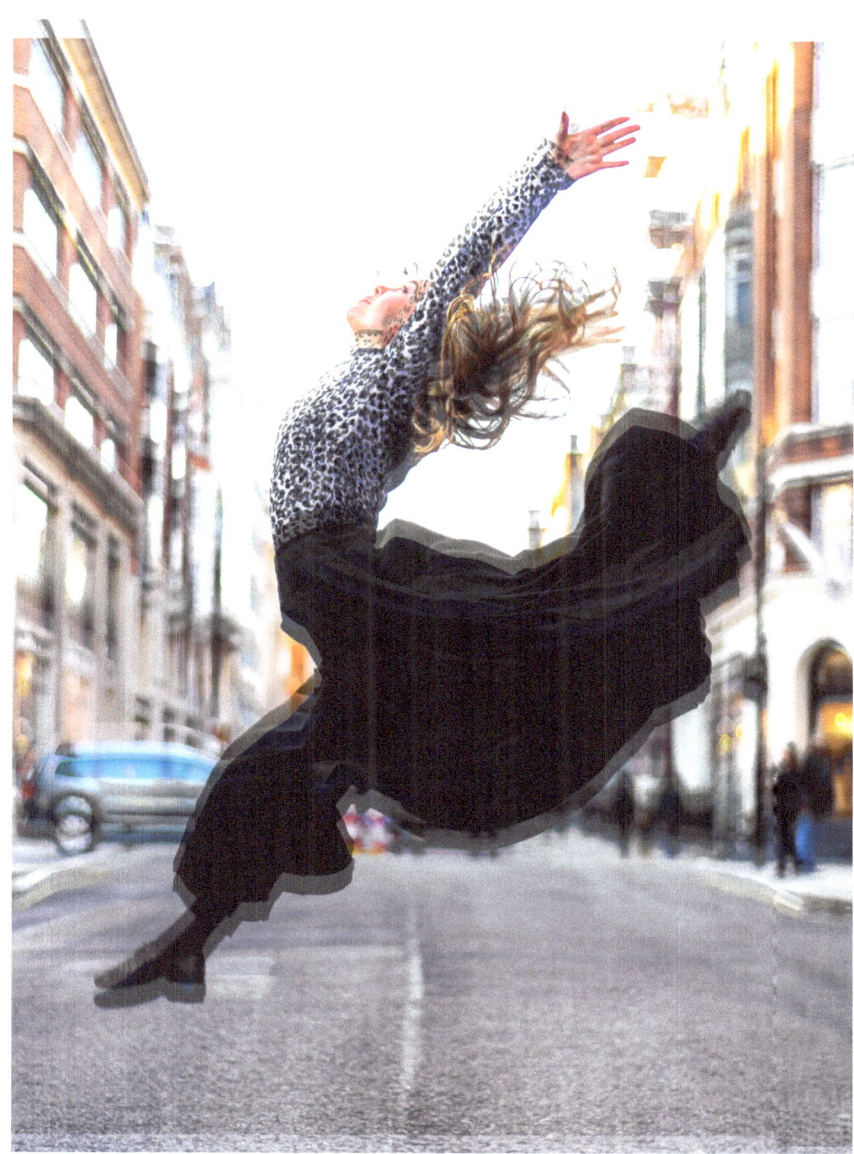

Untitled by Susi Petherick
The very lovely dancer Chelsea Louise Kester. Nikon D850 50mm lens ISO 100 1/250 sec at f1.8
Judged by Sarah Longes
Week 50

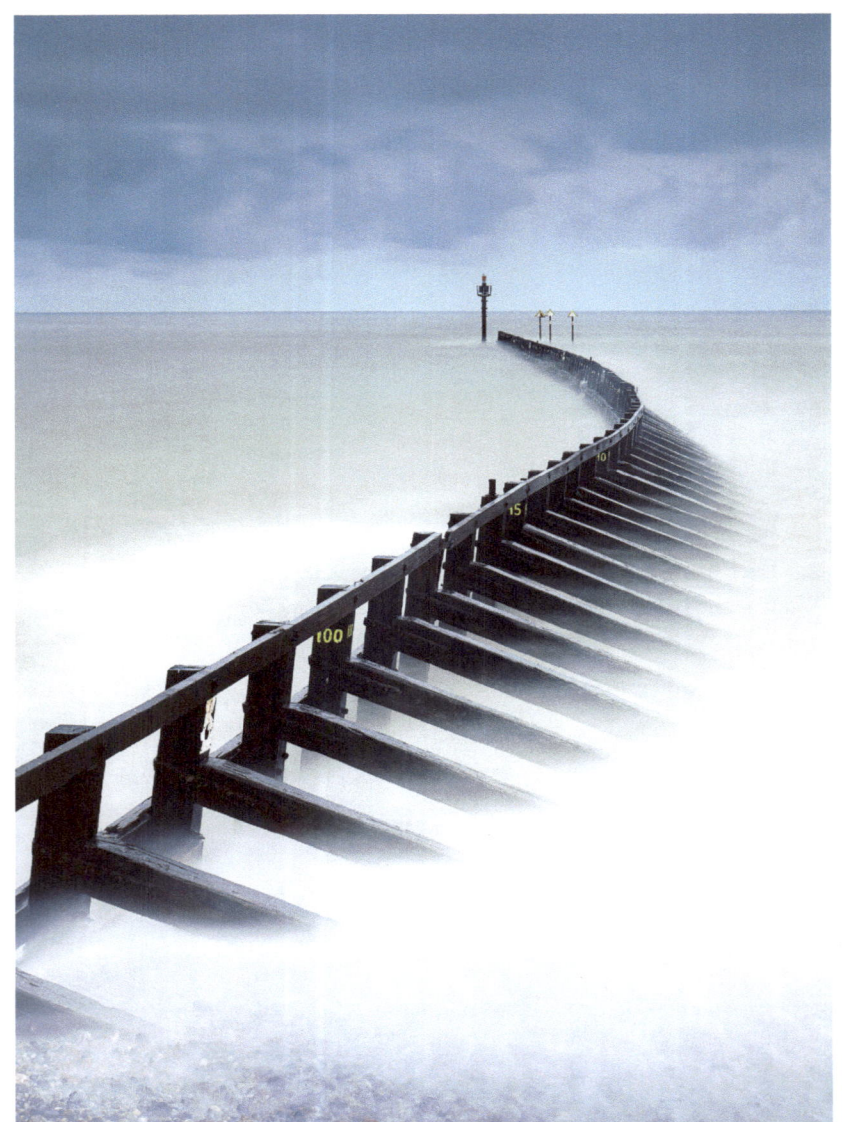

Timber Arc by Matthew Cattell

A beautiful timber structure that gently sweeps into the channel where the River Arun meets the sea.
Nikon D850, Nikon 24-70 f2.8 @ 65mm, f16, 25s and ISO65. Tripod, Polariser, 0.6 very hard grad, Little Stopper
Judged by Susi Petherick
Week 51

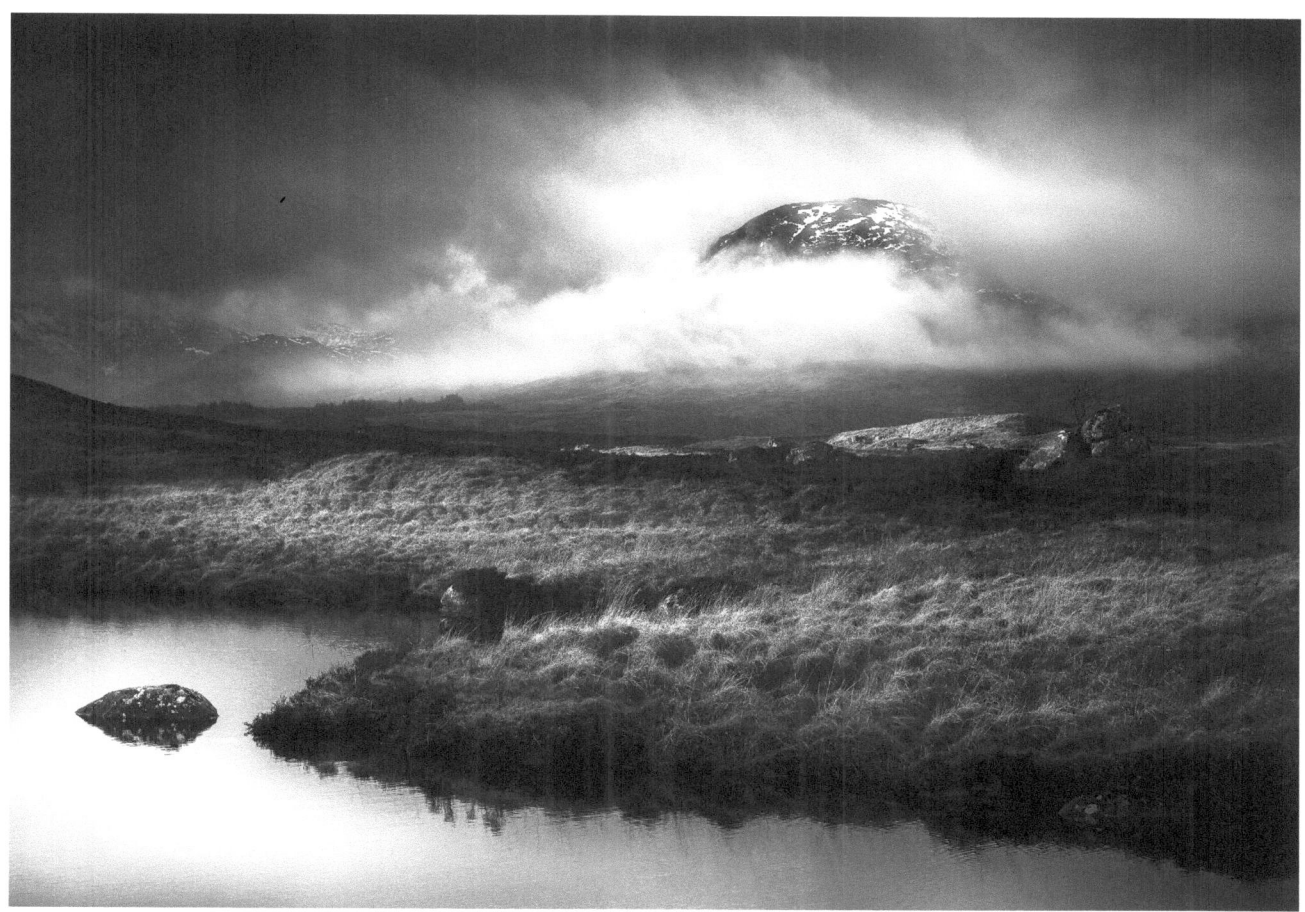

Patience by Matt McCormick

This image was taken on a rare outing during the festive period to Rannoch Moor. There was a lot of low cloud/mist passing over the Black Mount range and light was bursting through, lighting up the foreground occasionally. I decided to be patient and find a composition. I then waited for an hour until the mountain finally appeared through the cloud and my patience was rewarded. I felt going black and white helped to capture the drama of the scene. Nikon D750, Tamron 70-200 f/2.8 G2 @ f11 , 1/40 sec, IS0 100

Judged by Matthew Cattell

Week 52

Contributing Photographers Twitter Feeds

Week 1 - Claire Ashmore @claire_ashmore
Week 2 - Darren Rose @winterrosephoto
Week 3 & 12 - Will Mallett @will_mallett
Week 4 - James Benwell @JimPanda
Week 5, 10, 25 & 44 - Amar Sood @asPhotoUK
Week 6 - Anita Nicholson @AnitaNicholson
Week 7 - Daniel Sands @sndsphotography
Week 8 & 51 - Matthew Cattell @CattellMT
Week 9 - Dylan Nardini @ShuttRelease
Week 11, 38 & 49 - Sarah Longes @MiradorDesign
Week 13 & 19 - Stu Meech @stumeech
Week 14 - Glenys Garnett @ggcimages
Week 15 - Phil Savoie @PhilShoots
Week 16 - Amy Bateman @Croftfoot
Week 17 - Andrew Robertson @AndrewRPhoto1
Week 18 - Mandy Davies @Mand_davies5
Week 20 - Ian Lewis @IanLPhotography
Week 21 & 34 - Jay Birmingham @Jay_B_Photos
Week 22 - Pete Wilkinson @PeteWphoto
Week 23 - Keith Trueman @KeithTrueman
Week 24 - Paul Howell @bowerdaleu
Week 26 - Tom Lowe @f22digital
Week 27 & 43 - Jo Stephen @JoAnnunaki
Week 28 - Neil Moran @OnClearDaysUK
Week 29 - Stuart Sly @picturesbystu
Week 30 - Shaun Mills @therseamilsy
Week 31 - Martin Tosh @ToshMartin
Week 32 - Tony Sellen @TS46photo
Week 33 - Ashley Groom @Groomsickle
Week 35 - David Rippin @dmrippin
Week 36 - Jason Hudson @Edenphotograph1
Week 37 - Alistair Jones @ajones27
Week 39 - Elke Epp @ElkeEpp
Week 40 - Simon Watling @simonwatling
Week 41 - Gareth Mon Jones @gazmon1980
Week 42 - Andy Luddington @AndyLuddington
Week 45 - Dan Portch @danportch
Week 46 - Ollie Pocock @flyingsailor87
Week 47 - Neil Burnell @njburnell
Week 48 - Chaitanya Deshpande @chaitdesh
Week 50 - Susi Petherick @SusiPetherick
Week 52 - Matt McCormick @Mattosanfoto

www.sharemondays.co.uk
Produced by Dylan Nardini

www.ingramcontent.com/pod-product-compliance
Lightning Source LLC
Chambersburg PA
CBHW051923210526
45473CB00006B/2111